T0328607

Cambridge Elements

Elements in Reinventing Capitalism
edited by
Arie Y. Lewin
Duke University, The Fuqua School of Business
Till Talaulicar
University of Erfurt, Germany

TAMING CORPORATE POWER IN THE 21ST CENTURY

Gerald F. Davis
University of Michigan

ADAM SMITH
PANMURE
HOUSE

CAMBRIDGE
UNIVERSITY PRESS

CAMBRIDGE
UNIVERSITY PRESS

University Printing House, Cambridge CB2 8BS, United Kingdom

One Liberty Plaza, 20th Floor, New York, NY 10006, USA

477 Williamstown Road, Port Melbourne, VIC 3207, Australia

314–321, 3rd Floor, Plot 3, Splendor Forum, Jasola District Centre,
New Delhi – 110025, India

103 Penang Road, #05–06/07, Visioncrest Commercial, Singapore 238467

Cambridge University Press is part of the University of Cambridge.

It furthers the University's mission by disseminating knowledge in the pursuit of
education, learning, and research at the highest international levels of excellence.

www.cambridge.org
Information on this title: www.cambridge.org/9781009095426
DOI: 10.1017/9781009091664

First published 2022

A catalogue record for this publication is available from the British Library.

ISBN 978-1-009-09542-6 Paperback
ISSN 2634-8950 (online)
ISSN 2634-8942 (print)

Taming Corporate Power in the 21st Century

Elements in Reinventing Capitalism

DOI: 10.1017/9781009091664
First published online: April 2022

Gerald F. Davis
University of Michigan
Author for correspondence: Gerald F. Davis, gfdavis@umich.edu

Abstract: There is a broad consensus across the political spectrum in the United States that monopolistic corporations – particularly Big Tech companies – have grown too powerful, and that we need to revive antitrust to take on the "curse of bigness." But both the diagnosis and the cure are rooted in an outdated understanding of how the American economy is organized. Information and communication technologies have fundamentally altered the markets for capital, labor, supplies, and distribution in ways that undermine the basic categories we use to understand the economy. Nationality, industry, firm, size, employee, and other fundamental terms are increasingly detached from the operations of the economy. If we want to understand and tame the new sources of economic power, we need a new diagnosis and a new set of tools.

Keywords: corporate power, monopoly, digital revolution, shareholder capitalism, Big Tech

ISBNs: 9781009095426 (PB), 9781009091664 (OC)
ISSNs: 2634-8950 (online), 2634-8942 (print)

Contents

1 Introduction

"I'm using Robinhood on my Android to trade Dogecoin, which is a meme-based sarcastic cryptocurrency."

Imagine explaining this sentence to someone in 1990, before the Web, internet memes, smartphones, apps, and cryptocurrency. Now imagine explaining it to the 1890 US Congress that passed the Sherman Act.

Corporate power is out of control. Despite widespread political polarization in the United States, there is a surprisingly broad consensus on this one issue. Senators Josh Hawley and Amy Klobuchar agree with populists on the left and the right: Big business has grown too big and needs to be brought to heel.

The Biden Administration made taming the undue power of giant corporations a central theme of its first year. In his sweeping executive order to rein in big business in July 2021, President Biden said, "A fair, open, and competitive marketplace has long been a cornerstone of the American economy, while excessive market concentration threatens basic economic liberties, democratic accountability, and the welfare of workers, farmers, small businesses, startups, and consumers."[1]

Big Tech is especially fearsome. Information technology has seeped into every moment of our existence, from the cameras that scan our faces as we walk down the street and the online services that deliver our groceries to the smartphone resting a few inches away as we sleep. How we work, how we play, how we connect, and how we know increasingly take place through tools created and controlled by a small set of unaccountable corporations in Silicon Valley and Seattle. The COVID-19 pandemic exacerbated our vital dependence on online technologies for basic daily activities – school, work, shopping, dining, visiting friends and family – leaving us at the mercy of a handful of peculiar tax-dodging billionaires.

There is also broad consensus on the cause of our ills: monopoly power. Industry after industry is dominated by a small number of giant corporations with little or no competition. Monopolists – companies with too big a share of their market – have a habit of underpaying their suppliers and workers, overcharging their customers, strangling current or future competitors, and using their unjust profits to buy off politicians and regulators. The proceeds of their monopolistic activities enrich the aristocrats who own giant corporations, handing political power to unaccountable elites who play by their own rules.

---

[1] The White House, 2021."Executive Order on Promoting Competition in the American Economy," www.whitehouse.gov/briefing-room/presidential-actions/2021/07/09/executive-order-on-promoting-competition-in-the-american-economy/.

How did we get here? According to the standard narrative, America's economic vibrancy in the twentieth century was protected by antitrust laws that promoted competition, limiting mergers among rivals and the sleazy tactics that allow big companies to dominate their industry. The cure for the "curse of bigness" was mercifully straightforward: cut giant corporations down to size using the tools of antitrust, limit growth through mergers, and encourage more markets and more competition. Unfortunately – according to the narrative – smooth-talking economists from Chicago managed to hijack the noble mission of antitrust during the 1970s and sent us down the path of monopoly. As President Biden put it, "over the last several decades, as industries have consolidated, competition has weakened in too many markets, denying Americans the benefits of an open economy and widening racial, income, and wealth inequality. Federal Government inaction has contributed to these problems, with workers, farmers, small businesses, and consumers paying the price" (The White House, 2021).

The rare consensus about the dangers of monopoly relies on a set of stylized facts about how the economy works. But the stylized facts are wrong. They come from a twentieth-century understanding of the economy that no longer fits the situation we are in now. Information and communication technologies (ICTs) have undermined the basic categories we use to describe the economy: firm, industry, employee, income, nationality, monopoly – even size – are all contentious. To say that one or two giant corporations unfairly dominate an American industry due to their outsized market share (a standard notion of monopoly) is to misunderstand how power works in the new economy. And if we get the diagnosis wrong, we will not get the cure right – it will be like trying to fix the carburetor on a Tesla.

Take Zoom, the videoconferencing platform that became pervasive overnight during the COVID-19 pandemic. The Zoom app was downloaded a half-billion times in 2020 and has 300 million daily users. Zoom single-handedly enabled the work-from-home economy for white collar workers, and many of us do not pass a single day without a Zoom call. It introduced major product improvements throughout the pandemic: the Zoom of February 2022 works very differently from the Zoom of February 2020. Is Zoom a giant corporation? As of July 2021 it had a stock market value of over $110 billion (comparable to Goldman Sachs and IBM), yet it has only 4,422 employees around the world and rents server space from Amazon and Oracle.[2] What industry is it in, and who does it compete with – videoconferencing (so Google, Apple, Facebook,

---

[2] United States Securities and Exchange Commission, www.sec.gov/ix?doc=/Archives/edgar/data/1585521/000158552121000048/zm-20210131.htm.

Microsoft, Cisco), telecommunications (add in AT&T and Verizon), or something broader? Would we be better off if Zoom had more mutually incompatible competitors with slightly different versions of its features? (Those who have to endure meetings on Teams or Webex or Meet/Hangout etc. know the answer.) How did a tiny company with few employees and rented assets beat the most unscrupulous monopolists of our time? And would it make any difference if Zoom was incorporated in Ireland (like Accenture and Medtronic), or owned by a Chinese parent (like TikTok and Grindr)?

Over the past forty years, ICTs have enabled more expansive markets in successive domains, first for capital (financialization), then for supply (Nikefication), then distribution (Amazon), and, finally, labor (Uberization). Along the way, the purpose of the corporation was narrowed to one: creating shareholder value. A matrix of institutions grew up to enforce this purpose and to punish those who deviated. Far more than monopoly, this is the source of our societal ills: The rules of the game under shareholder capitalism favor profit, whatever its source and whatever its consequence for society. Sometimes monopoly helps corporations create shareholder value, but it is only one tool among many. And as long as the business sector is dominated by the idea that corporations exist to create shareholder value, altering the rules of competition will not make the economy more humane, democratic, or sustainable.

The digital transformation of business is changing the shape of the American economy in unpredictable ways. How companies recruit labor, capital, and supplies, how they distribute their products, and how they manage their people and operations are all metamorphosing, creating new opportunities and new hazards. The basic architecture of enterprise today looks radically different from a generation ago, and even different from the start of 2020, when the COVID-19 pandemic began. Work-from-home will inevitably lead to a greater use of global contractors rather than local employees, and we are increasingly seeing "placeless" businesses that assemble and manage their components entirely online. When Coinbase went public in April 2021, its prospectus listed no physical headquarters address and noted that it was a "remote-first" enterprise.[3] And after Proposition 22 in California,[4] we are likely to see even more frontline work done by app-based gig workers (delivery drivers, warehouse laborers, kitchen staff) recruited by the task or by the shift, their daily wages subject to the whim of the market.

More markets and more competition are not the solution to every problem, and sometimes giant scale has its advantages. Walmart, the scourge of the

---

[3] United States Securities and Exchange Commission, www.sec.gov/Archives/edgar/data/1679788/000162828021003168/coinbaseglobalincs-1.htm.

[4] Athreya (2021) details the post-election trajectory of Proposition 22.

anti-monopolists, has the monopsony power to force its biggest suppliers to reduce their carbon emissions, to stock energy-efficient light bulbs at a sufficiently massive scale to make them cost effective for its customers, to get affordable organic groceries into thousands of stores, and to put solar panels on roofs across America.[5] No coalition of Main Street retailers could accomplish this so rapidly. (Walmart also had the power to force suppliers to meet its "China price," driving down the wages of workers at its biggest providers.[6]) Or consider health care affordability. The governmental equivalent of Walmart (say, Medicare For All) could quickly drive down the price of medicines by surpassing the bargaining power of pharmaceutical companies, streamlining unnecessary paperwork, and coordinating care across geographies. Big companies and big government can be bullies, but sometimes it is beneficial to have bullies on your side – if they can be made democratically accountable. And more competition is not always the right answer. The opioid crisis will not be solved with more competitors for Purdue and Insys. The obesity epidemic will not be fixed with even more producers of hyperprocessed food. And in a world hurtling toward climate collapse, we don't need more petroleum companies, airlines, or meatpackers spewing more greenhouse gases into the atmosphere.

The challenges we face are on the same scale as the shift from agriculture to manufacturing around the turn of the twentieth century when the modern corporation took over the economy. But we can't simply rely on the same tools we did then. In an age when all our human transactions and relationships are intermediated online, reviving twentieth-century antitrust is not sufficient. We need a new understanding of the place of business and government in organizing the economy so that it is democratically accountable and serves human needs. My aim here is to provide a starting point.

This Element is a short take on a big topic. In Section 2 I describe the digital transformation of business and how ICTs have transformed how companies access the raw ingredients of business – capital, labor, supplies, and distribution – in ways that favor the use of markets. Increasingly, the parts needed to create a business are available online, ready to snap together like a set of Legos, which helps explain the long-term decline in the number of public corporations in the United States.[7] In Section 3, I discuss the new anti-monopoly movement and its diagnosis of our current era. From the Sherman Act of 1890 until the 1950s, the US Congress guided corporations to behave themselves by regulating how they compete with each other and engage with their suppliers

---

[5] See Barbaro (2007) and Plambeck and Denend (2008).

[6] Wilmers (2018) describes the supplier wage effects of Walmart's monopsony power.

[7] "Public corporations" are companies listed on a stock market like the New York Stock Exchange. See Davis (2016a, 2016b) on the decline of the public corporation and the rise of alternatives.

(primarily during the Progressive Era) and by regulating the capital and labor markets during the New Deal era. This limited the "curse of bigness" and aligned what's good for business with what's good for society. But, according to the anti-monopolists, the curse that plagued the American economy at the turn of the twentieth century is back, brought about by a wrong turn in antitrust four decades ago. In response, they propose a revival of trustbusting. I break down how this diagnosis gets it wrong in Section 4, suggesting that it is not creeping monopoly but shareholder capitalism that got us into our current mess. Contrary to the monopoly narrative, there is little evidence that industry has become massively more concentrated since Reagan took office – but there is compelling proof of the hegemony of shareholder value as the North Star for corporate activities.

Technology has undermined some of the basic categories we use to understand the economy. Sections 5, 6, and 7 describe fundamental changes in three basic terms. *Nationality* seems fairly basic, but scores of US-based firms such as Apple, Google, and Netflix make most of their revenues overseas, many are incorporated outside the United States, and new virtual businesses undermine the very idea of "place." *Industry* was straightforward when the biggest businesses made steel or cars or they refined oil or operated railroads. Today, however, there is often a disjuncture between what companies do, what markets they operate in, and where their revenues come from. The "technology" industry ends up encompassing businesses that operate in nearly every market, from hotels and restaurants to transportation and construction to national security, which makes it tough to define terms like market share. Finally, *size* is an increasingly unhelpful metaphor to describe corporations as revenues, employment, assets, and market capitalization are increasingly uncorrelated. Corporations with minimal assets and employees can have vast market caps (e.g., Netflix, Zoom); enormous employers can have petite valuations (e.g., the retailers Kroger, Walgreens, Albertsons), as can those with world-beating revenues (drug middlemen McKesson and AmerisourceBergen). The "curse of bigness" is too blunt a term to be useful today because we no longer agree on what *bigness* is. If nationality, industry, and size elude easy definition, then identifying monopoly power in a rigorous way will be even more troubled, no matter what the public consensus may be. As the judge who threw out the Federal Trade Commission's (FTC) initial filing of an antitrust case against Facebook put it,

> It is almost as if the agency expects the court to simply nod to the conventional wisdom that Facebook is a monopolist . . . Yet, whatever it may mean to the public, "monopoly power" is a term of art under federal law with a precise

economic meaning: the power to profitably raise prices or exclude competition in a properly defined market. (Kang, 2021)

The American dream of starting a business and being your own boss is still alive, and all the parts a business needs are available online – yet, paradoxically, business startup rates, by some measures, have been in a long-run downward spiral, albeit with a surprising upward blip during the COVID-19 pandemic. In Section 8, I unpack the myth of entrepreneurship and highlight the dangers of using the rhetoric of self-employment to cloak an increasingly precarious employment relation. Finally, in Section 9, I dive into what comes next. A buffet of policy options has been proposed to take on the new monopolies, from more vigorous antitrust enforcement to a new regulatory agency for digital platforms. I end by considering the bigger stakes we need to consider when we rein in the new economy, and why we need to put democracy first.

2 The Digital Transformation of Business

Suppose you came up with a brilliant invention that would make life easier for busy people – say, a computerized pressure cooker that allowed home chefs to throw raw ingredients into a pot, push some buttons, and come back an hour later to a healthy dinner. How would you turn that into a business?

To create a working prototype, you might have to buy some capital equipment. Perhaps you have rich friends or family who could lend you some money. If the product you develop is viable and your market research is solid, you might ask a bank for a loan to build a factory and hire skilled workers. You'd need to retain a sales force to get stores like Sears and JCPenney to stock your product, and a shipping company to distribute it. As sales grew, you might hire more workers and expand your factory. If you got big enough, you might even list shares on a stock market to fund your expansion. Within a few years, or decades, you might grow the business into a lasting legacy, a pillar of your local community.

At least, that's what you would have done forty years ago. Today, after you created your initial design sketch, you might recruit some freelance designers on Upwork to perfect your idea. You could raise funding for your venture on Indiegogo – but you might not need much. Alibaba lists scores of factories waiting to manufacture your product once you have design specifications that you can send over the Internet.[8] And Amazon is happy to advertise and distribute your product to customers and collect their payments. (If your product is really popular, they might even compliment your business by creating an

---

[8] Dozens of low-cost Instant Pot knockoffs can be found at www.alibaba.com/showroom/electric-pressure-cooker.html.

Amazon-branded knockoff, produced by the same manufacturer, that undercuts your price.)

This is, more or less, the story of the Instant Pot. Robert Wang, an Ontario computer science PhD who was out of work after the 2008 financial crisis, along with two other engineers, spent eighteen months perfecting a design for a versatile, low-cost, computerized pressure cooker, funded by $350,000 of his savings. After its debut on Amazon in 2010, Wang sent 200 Instant Pots to influential food bloggers and chefs, who shared positive evaluations (and, crucially, Instant Pot-specific recipes) online. Thanks to a cascade of rapturous reviews on Amazon, the product went viral and grew a large cult following. Hundreds of Instant Pot cookbooks have been published for every kind of cuisine, and thousands of recipes are posted online. Distribution was handed off to Fulfillment By Amazon, which received the products directly from the factory in China, packed them, and shipped them to customers. Product research consisted of reading the many thousands of reviews on Amazon and updating the appliance based on user experiences. By 2018, the Instant Pot was selling 300,000 units on Amazon's Prime Day alone – all from a company with just 50 employees in Ottawa. No advertising, no factories, few employees, and almost no assets – yet the Instant Pot had become a global phenomenon.[9]

The Instant Pot story demonstrates that the American dream is still alive and well – in Ontario, Canada. The bigger lesson of Instant Pot is about the digital transformation of business. Information and communication technologies have transformed every aspect of how business is done over the past generation. In the words of Marc Andreessen, "Software is eating the world," and that applies to all the core components for creating an enterprise (Andreessen, 2011). They have reshaped the basic raw materials for building a company – just as structural steel, reinforced concrete, and plate glass changed buildings in cities around the world over a century ago.

Because software is "eating the world," markets are eating the world, too. Information and communication technologies have changed how companies raise capital (hello Indiegogo, Robinhood, and Coinbase), find suppliers (Alibaba), recruit labor (Uber, DoorDash, Mturk, Upwork), and distribute their products and services (Amazon, Shopify). They have also changed how firms operate internally, as employees (or contractors) are increasingly supervised by algorithms, not human managers. In a world where any kid in a dorm room can assemble a business from online parts, the corporation itself is increasingly becoming an obsolete way to organize economic activity. This helps explain why there are half as many corporations listed on the stock market

---

[9] For details on the Instant Pot story, see Montag (2017) and Roose (2017).

as there were twenty-five years ago.[10] It's as if the National Basketball Association (NBA) were replaced by impromptu pickup games, all over the economy.

The core factor markets that make up a corporation have changed in parallel ways in recent years due to ICTs. In the United States, the recurring theme across all these markets is the same: ICTs enable markets for things that were previously too complicated or too costly to trade on markets, leading companies to outsource rather than doing things internally. As Nobel economist Ronald Coase (1937) would put it, ICTs are driving down the transaction costs of using online markets for inputs. More and more, it's cheaper to buy (or perhaps more aptly, to rent) than to make. This transformation has happened successively across markets for capital (financialization), supplies (Nikefication), distribution (Amazon), and labor (Uberization), and is changing practices inside the business as well.

2.1 Financialization: How Capital Markets Spread from Wall Street to the Parking Meters on Your Street

Over the past forty years, financing for business has increasingly taken place through markets rather than institutions like banks. And even if you do pass through a marble bank lobby to take out a mortgage or a business loan, the odds are good that the loan will be resold, bundled, and sliced into bonds before you make it out the door (a process known as "securitization").

Financialization is what happens when financial markets become central to the operations of the economy.[11] Thanks to ICTs, financial markets have spread broadly around the world and deeply into the economy. Dozens of countries opened stock exchanges over the past four decades, enabling global investors to invest in distant markets and to fund ventures that might have been beyond the reach of domestic savers.[12] Kids waiting for the school bus with their smartphones may be trading emerging market Exchange Traded Funds (ETFs) or GameStop options on Robinhood. And almost anything with a reliable cash flow has been securitized, from college loans and sitcom royalties to life insurance payoffs of the elderly and future collections from parking meters.

The most familiar form of securitization is the home mortgage market. For generations, people seeking to buy a house might take out a thirty-year mortgage from a local bank, which funded the mortgage through the deposit accounts of local savers. In the early 1970s, government-sponsored organizations in the

---

[10] See Davis (2016b) on the vanishing American public corporation.

[11] Davis and Kim (2015) trace the history of financialization.

[12] Weber et al. (2009) describe the global spread of stock exchanges after 1980.

United States pioneered the practice of buying mortgages from banks, thus freeing up the banks' capital to make more loans. Hundreds of mortgages were pooled and resold as bonds, to be paid with the proceeds from the loans. Any single loan might be more or less risky, but a pool of loans becomes predictable (at least, before 2007). Over a two-decade period the mortgage value chain fragmented from a single bank into a sequence of specialists – brokers who worked directly with customers, mortgage banks who originated the loans, securitizers who bundled them into bonds, and servicers who subsequently managed the loans.[13] This was largely enabled by ICTs such as the fax machine, the spreadsheet, electronic credit ratings, and scoring algorithms that encouraged standardization.

Anyone who has seen the movie *The Big Short* may have noticed finance nerds looking over spreadsheets in which each row was a home mortgage and each column a piece of information (the homeowner's credit score and payment history, the selling price of the house, the interest rate being charged, and so on). A simple but indispensable technology that everyone has access to today – the spreadsheet – allowed securitizers, rating agencies, and buyers to estimate how much income is likely to flow into that pool. Now take that same idea and apply it to credit card receivables, student loans, business loans, tobacco lawsuit settlements, future collections on toll roads – if there is an income stream (an "asset"), someone on Wall Street has turned it into an asset-backed security. And if you can easily share the information on that spreadsheet (say, as an email attachment), there might be a market for it. You might even find kids on Robinhood to buy your viatical bonds (backed by the life insurance payoffs of the elderly).[14]

For business, this means that there are many more ways to access finance than bank loans, and even these loans are likely to be resold and diced up into bonds. Any separation between commercial banking (making loans) and investment banking (underwriting and trading securities) has effectively evaporated: It's all markets now.

2.2 Nikefication: Why Nothing You Buy Is Made by the Company on the Label Any More

The sneaker company Nike pioneered an ingenious business model in which it designed and marketed its shoes but left it to East Asian contractors to do the actual manufacturing. Nike was in the branding business, not the production business. In the 1990s, this asset-lite model, common in the garment industry,

---

[13] Jacobides (2005) traces the history of the mortgage market and its deverticalization.
[14] Davis (2010) provides detail on the rise of securitization.

began to spread to almost every manufacturing industry, from simple goods like sneakers and T-shirts to highly complex products like laptop computers. Apple once prided itself on its world-class production facilities in Silicon Valley; now its goods are made by Foxconn and other remote vendors. Nikefication is not just in manufacturing, as American corporations entrust their payroll to ADP, their IT to Infosys, their pension plan to Fidelity, their job design to Accenture, their server space to Amazon Web Services, and more.

The creation of the World Wide Web in the 1990s greatly accelerated this process by making it possible for companies to comparison-shop for suppliers, even in geographies and time zones far from home. In 1937, Ronald Coase claimed that "the main reason why it is profitable to establish a firm would seem to be that there is a cost of using the price mechanism. The most obvious cost of 'organising' production through the price mechanism is that of discovering what the relevant prices are."[15] The World Wide Web greatly drove down the transaction costs of organizing production through the price mechanism, rendering it cheaper to buy inputs rather than make them internally.

Today it is possible to rent entire supply chains. If you have a recipe for tomato sauce or beer or pet food, a design for a sneaker or an evening gown, a concept for a flat-screen television or mobile phone handset, you can hire a vendor to make it for you, including managing their own supply chain. And while the 1990s was seen as the decade of outsourcing, the years following 2001 when China joined the World Trade Organization accelerated this trend. In January 2001, the "Computer and Electronic Products" industry in the United States employed 1.9 million people. Three years later, it was just 1.3 million. In a brief period, the industry had shrunk by nearly one-third. Meanwhile, anyone with an Internet connection can set electronics factories in motion in Shenzhen via Alibaba.

While this is easiest to visualize for clothing or food or consumer electronics, the basic Nike recipe – design internally, produce externally – is spreading to even the most traditional manufacturing industries, enabling surprising new entrants. The CEO of electric vehicle (EV) company Fisker, which went public in the fall of 2020, stated: "We're not going to do our own manufacturing. It would be stupid for any EV startup to make a brand-new factory" (DeBord, 2021). Instead, it will rely on contract manufacturer Magna and, of course, Foxconn, to produce its vehicles (DeBord, 2021).

2.3 Fullfilled by Amazon ... Very Fulfilled

Since its launch in 1994, Amazon has grown to be a universal distribution channel. As we saw with Instant Pot, Amazon can take customer orders, receive inventory

---

[15] See Coase (1937) for the initial statement on transaction costs as the rationale for firms.

directly from the factory, pack it up, and deliver it to the customer's front door. The complete service is called "Fulfillment by Amazon." Of course, Amazon is not the only vendor who offers this service, but it is the most comprehensive.

Because of its "universal distribution" approach, Amazon has completed the circuit of the virtual business model, allowing online merchants to sell products that they never touch. This has created a kaleidoscopic shopping experience, as consumers are presented with highly-rated brands with bizarre names like Nertpow, SHSTFD, MAJCF ... seemingly christened by a cat walking across a keyboard (Herrman, 2020)

Moreover, the Amazon platform enables a business model in which an entrepreneur can scan the market for products with a high markup, create a lower-priced knockoff design, find a vendor on Alibaba to produce it, and claim their perch on Amazon. As *New York Times* writer Farhad Manjoo put it, "We're going to get better products for ludicrously low prices, and big brands across a range of categories – the Nests and Netgears of the world – are going to find it harder than ever to get us to shell out big money for their wares" (Manjoo, 2017). For the single most central device someone owns – their smartphone – consumers may be willing to shell out a premium price for an Apple product. But for the dozens of other product categories they buy each year, they may not have to.

2.4 Uberization: Why You Can Now Get a Taxi, a Massage, or a Doctor's House Call on Your Phone

The last market to succumb to ICTs was the labor market. There is something special about labor that makes it unlike capital, supplies, and distribution, a fact that is recognized in American employment law. But ICT-driven changes in the labor market are drastically changing the nature of employment.

If you haven't looked for a job lately, you may be surprised to discover how recruitment is done these days. Many hiring companies rely on outside services like Indeed.com to deliver them a passel of potential recruits. Prospective employees upload their résumé, flag the kinds of jobs they are interested in, and await alerts for openings. An employer might ask them to record their answers to a few interview questions via their phone video, allowing hiring managers to preview potential workers and, if they choose, to proffer employment along with details of the job. At the fancier end of the spectrum, employers might use Hirevue, "Your end-to-end Hiring Experience Platform with video interview software, conversational AI, and assessments."[16] Some services helpfully incorporate algorithms purported to read emotions and personality

---

[16] www.hirevue.com/ (accessed July 20, 2021).

traits from video interviews to screen out those who are too anxious, or too relaxed, or too different from the preferred demographic.

Once employed, workers can be scheduled, managed, evaluated, and fired using Workforce Management Systems software. Those working from home may find that their employer requires them to leave their camera on at all times, and to endure keystroke tracking and frequent screen captures throughout the workday. Over the course of the COVID-19 pandemic, the degree and forms of intrusive monitoring by employers have reached truly Kafkaesque levels of invasiveness – something unlikely to recede even as people return to in-person work (Abril and Harwell, 2021). Amazon, always in the vanguard, has upped the ante with onboard AI-powered cameras that monitor and score their delivery drivers continuously and chide them in real time for perceived missteps (e.g., not maintaining a safe distance) (Gurley, 2021).

Across a broad range of industries, employees are being replaced by contractors. Uberization is

> "the creation of spot labor markets enabled by smartphones in which buyers and sellers can connect for the performance of specific tasks. The most visible version of Uberization is the ridehailing industry, where riders and drivers are connected via a smartphone app. But the idea is more generic: as the cliche goes, there is an Uber for everything now, from food delivery and Ikea furniture assembly to virtual physician house calls" (Davis and Sinha, 2021).

Uberization marks the transition from an employment relation – a protected tie between workers and companies – to a contractor relation. It is a shift from jobs to tasks, and it is increasingly pervasive across all levels of skill, from dog walking to diagnosing X-rays. In 2019 Google had 102,000 employees but 121,000 temps, vendors, and contractors (TVCs) – in other words, most of the workforce was made up of disposable TVCs, not employees (Wakabayashi, 2019).

While contract work and spot labor markets have existed for a long time, GPS-enabled smartphones greatly reduce the transaction costs of hiring work by the task. It is easy to imagine a scenario in which qualified workers bid for tasks or shifts, with low bidders setting the wage rate for the day. Freed from archaic concepts like the "job" and the "minimum wage," wages would rise and fall day-to-day, and even hour-to-hour, according to market conditions – perhaps with a quality adjustment for those who have not angered their AI overseer.

While this sounds fanciful and vaguely dystopian, it is already underway. In November 2020, after California voters approved Proposition 22, which allowed Uber, Lyft, DoorDash, and similar firms to classify their laborers as contractors and not employees, several California grocery companies fired their delivery drivers and switched to app-based services (Harnett, 2021). Restaurants are already hiring kitchen staff by the shift using apps such as Pared, and UberWorks launched in 2019 to create a platform for companies to hire labor of all types by the shift (Talbot, 2019).[17]

One of the implications of this new system, in which labor is evaluated and hired (or not) by the shift, is that workers bear the transaction costs that employers have sloughed off, spending hours in the evening and at weekends polishing up their LinkedIn profile and scrapping for gigs. The famous motto of Uber founder Travis Kalanick – "Always be hustling" – is an apt description of a way of life in which leisure hours are spent taking online courses, networking, and smiling for the AI bot that will evaluate your job application.[18]

These trends were well underway when the COVID-19 pandemic hit and accelerated them all. The year 2020 will be marked by historians as the moment when the digitalization of the economy made a decade's progress in a single year. As a result, in the years to come we are likely to see a lot more businesses that look like Instant Pot, and a lot fewer that look like General Motors. We have shifted from the world of professional hockey – with specialized equipment and arenas, stable teams and schedules, and reliable records of how the competition went – to the world of pickup basketball.

Of course, not all industries will end up in a situation where large corporations are replaced by pop-up networks that look like the "maker" of the Instant Pot. Apple, Amazon, and Alphabet have many years left in them, and someone needs to operate those massive server farms (although their hands-on employment is quite minimal). Generic factories manufacturing mobile phones, electric cars, and tomato sauce are also operated by ongoing corporations – although these, again, are likely to be highly automated, employee-lite enterprises. More significantly, the technological changes enabling markets are embraced far more fervently in the United States than anywhere else. While there is an Uber for everything in America, in many countries Uber's business model simply won't work because of local laws and customs. The smartphone-enabled ridehailing industry looks vastly different in Germany and Sweden than in the United States, and even more distinct in Nigeria, Indonesia, India, and China.[19] America's business climate is unique, and the institutional climate change wrought by ICTs will look different according to local conditions. Just

---

[17] The company apparently closed UberWorks the following May; see Staffing Industry Analysts (2021).

[18] For a detailed and disturbing ethnography of how the new labor market is playing out in California, see the Institute for the Future's report "California Worker Voices: Anticipating the Future from the Frontlines"; www.iftf.org/caworkervoices.

[19] See Thelen (2018) on Germany, Sweden, and the US, and Davis and Sinha (2021) for Nigeria, Indonesia, China, and India.

because a technology creates the possibility for a new kind of market does not mean that the market will emerge – at least outside the United States.

3 Rising Monopoly Power and a New Gilded Age?

Antitrust is back in fashion. Across the political spectrum in the United States, there is rising concern that corporate power has become too concentrated, threatening the fairness of the economy and perhaps even democracy itself. You know something is happening when Josh Hawley, right-wing Republican senator from Missouri, and Amy Klobuchar, liberal Democratic senator from Minnesota, both publish books about smashing monopolies at the same time. Big Tech firms such as Facebook, Google, and Amazon are the subjects of antitrust lawsuits at the state and federal level, and the Biden Administration has stocked up on activist antitrust scholars and launched a broad campaign against corporate monopoly power. It has been over a century since America has seen this kind of consensus about the dangers of corporate concentration.

Dozens of recent books and articles argue that we are living through a new Gilded Age, just as we did at the turn of the twentieth century. Their diagnosis echoes that of Teddy Roosevelt, the original trustbuster, over a century ago: Corporations have grown too big and have used their wealth and power to corrupt politics and unjustly enrich an elite class of robber barons and Wall Street bankers at the expense of the common person.[20]

Underlying all this concern is monopoly power. According to the critics, monopolies are responsible for nearly all our ills as a society: low pay and economic inequality, bad health care and overpriced medicines, terrible service from cable companies and airlines, the collapse of journalism, the blandness of every downtown stocked with the same chain stores and restaurants, and the fact that kids spend all day staring at their phones and getting anxious and depressed. As Barry Lynn put it, "Whatever you are angry about, somewhere in the chain of blame you will almost always find a monopolist."[21]

These concerns reached their most powerful expression in an October 2020 Congressional subcommittee report that detailed the abuses dealt out by four tech giants: Google, Facebook, Amazon, and Apple. And they are setting the agenda for a renaissance in the regulation of business.

---

[20] The text of Roosevelt's "New Nationalism" speech of 1910, in which he laid out his case against corporate power, is available at https://obamawhitehouse.archives.gov/blog/2011/12/06/arch ives-president-teddy-roosevelts-new-nationalism-speech.

[21] Lynn (2020: 4).

3.1 The Corporatization of the American Economy and the Progressive Response

Around the turn of the twentieth century, the American economy was transformed from a regional to a national one through a vast merger wave engineered by Wall Street. The essential vehicle for this transformation was the corporation. In 1890 there were fewer than a dozen manufacturers listed on American stock markets, and the largest manufacturer – Carnegie Steel – was a limited partnership overseen by one man. By 1910, exchange-listed corporations increasingly dominated major industries, and Carnegie Steel had morphed into US Steel, the world's first billion-dollar corporation.[22]

A combination of economies of scale that reduced per-unit costs and ruthless competitive tactics meant that many industries were dominated by giant monopolies (e.g., Standard Oil, US Steel, American Tobacco) or oligopolies (General Electric and Westinghouse). The irony was that all this combination happened after the passage of the Sherman Act of 1890, which aimed at reining in the power of monopolies. The Sherman Act forbids companies from fixing prices, as the trusts had done. It further makes it illegal to acquire or maintain monopoly power through exclusionary conduct. Notably, being a monopoly (by having, say, a 90 percent market share) is not itself illegal – it is anticompetitive behavior that is forbidden. The text of the act is short and under-specified – the crucial part of Section II states: "Every person who shall monopolize, or attempt to monopolize, or combine or conspire with any other person or persons, to monopolize any part of the trade or commerce among the several States, or with foreign nations, shall be deemed guilty of a felony."[23] And it turns out there were many ways to "attempt to monopolize."

Despite the act's provisions, monopolies multiplied over the next two decades. The new giant corporations that followed the Sherman Act created problems for a democratic society. Monopolies could overcharge their customers, underpay their suppliers and employees, crush their competitors, and use their ill-gotten profits to buy political influence. A corporation that gained a stranglehold on a crucial transportation route, fuel, essential raw material, or means of communication, could use its leverage to mint dynastic fortunes, creating an aristocracy made up of robber barons. The Progressive movement arose in large part in response to this threat.

---

[22] See Chandler (1977) for the standard account of this movement and Lamoreaux (1985) and Roy (1999) for more critical accounts.

[23] Sherman Anti-Trust Act (1890), www.ourdocuments.gov/doc.php?flash=false&doc=51&page=transcript.

Who were these new giants? In 1912, the Dow Jones index included ten corporations that produced copper, lead, steel, rubber, leather, and sugar; a train car manufacturer; and General Electric (see Table 1). Note that these were not, just yet, the familiar pillars of the industrial economy: Ford did not introduce the moving assembly line until 1913, and giant mass-production factories had not conquered industry.

To put the threat of monopoly in context: In 1912 the United States had no income tax, no estate tax, no Department of Labor, no Federal Reserve, and no FTC. US Steel's assets were larger than the annual budget of the US federal government. America had a regulatory system fit for a regional agricultural economy at a point when it was becoming an urbanized industrial powerhouse. (Meanwhile, across the ocean the great powers included the Austro–Hungarian Empire, the Ottoman Empire, and the Russian Empire – all of which would vanish before the end of the decade.)

The presidential election of 1912 was in part a referendum on how to limit or channel the power of these new behemoths. All the major candidates (Woodrow Wilson, Teddy Roosevelt, William Howard Taft, and Eugene V. Debs) agreed that corporate power was a problem; they differed, primarily, on how government should respond. Roosevelt believed that in industries with economies of scale, big corporations were economically inevitable and should be tamed by a powerful federal government – in essence, an economy of regulated monopolies. Wilson and his advisors believed that their size alone was a threat that should be dealt with by keeping businesses as dispersed as was feasible. The 1911 breakups of Standard Oil and American Tobacco exemplified the kind of action Wilson favored.

Wilson won that election, and during the first two years of his administration the United States gained new powers to keep industries competitive. The Clayton Act of 1914 extended the Sherman Act by explicitly forbidding several anticompetitive actions: mergers that lessen competition; sharing board members among competing companies; price discrimination; and exclusive dealings

Table 1 The Dow Jones index, 1912

Amalgamated Copper	Central Leather	US Rubber
American Car and Foundry	General Electric	US Rubber pfd.
American Smelting and Refining	National Lead	US Steel
American Sugar	Peoples Gas Light and Coke	US Steel pfd.

and tying. The Clayton Act was much more explicit than the Sherman Act in specifying what companies could and could not do, although it also created room for interpretation by the Department of Justice and the new FTC.

Much of the thinking behind this approach to regulation came from Louis Brandeis, who Wilson appointed to the Supreme Court in 1916. Brandeis saw industries as tending naturally toward greater concentration and monopoly, and he recognized the threat that such concentrated economic power could pose to a democracy. In a Brandeisian world, small is both beautiful and better for democracy.

3.2 The New Deal and the Regulation of Capital and Labor Markets

The laws created to limit corporate power and monopolistic abuses during the Progressive Era were expanded during the New Deal that followed the election of Franklin D. Roosevelt in 1932. Where the Sherman Act and the Clayton Act created rules governing competition in product markets and supplier markets, New Deal reforms took on capital markets and labor markets.

By this time, the composition of the leading corporations had shifted from the production of raw materials to manufacturing and other advanced industries (see Table 2) and the economic threats came less from concentrated product markets than from powerful finance and weak labor.

In finance, there were new laws to keep banks dispersed and to maintain separation between investment banking (underwriting and trading in stocks and bonds) and commercial banking (taking in deposits and making loans to business). The 1933 Banking Act (the Glass–Steagall Act) created deposit insurance, prohibited banks from risky speculation with depositors' money, and prevented commercial banks from combining with investment banks. The long-term success of the project to subdue the power of banks is shown by the

Table 2 The Dow Jones index, 1932

Allied Chemical	General Electric	Nash Motors
American Can	General Foods	Procter & Gamble
American Smelting	General Motors	Sears Roebuck
American Tobacco	Goodyear	Standard Oil CA (Chevron)
Bethlehem Steel	IBM	Standard Oil NJ (Exxon)
Borden	International Harvester	Texas Company (Texaco)
Chrysler	International Nickel	Union Carbide
Coca-Cola	International Shoe	US Steel
Drug Inc.	Johns Manville	Westinghouse
Eastman Kodak	Loew's	Woolworth

fact that by 1980 the United States had 12,000 commercial banks, nearly all limited to branching within a single state.[24] It also had thousands of local savings and loans, credit unions, asset finance firms, check cashing stores, and more. By contrast, Canada had a half-dozen major national banks at that time, and German banking was dominated by three major "universal banks" (that is, institutions that did both investment banking and lending).

The 1933 Securities Act created federal regulation for companies that issued stocks and bonds, and it required corporations to disclose systematic financial information to their investors. The 1934 Securities Exchange Act created the Securities and Exchange Commission (SEC) to oversee trading in securities and to implement the disclosure requirements in the 1933 act. These two acts are the reason we have such comprehensive financial information about corporations listed on American markets.

For labor, Congress vouchsafed the right of workers to form unions via the Wagner Act of 1935, which created the National Labor Relations Board to oversee the process of organizing and collective bargaining. The Fair Labor Standards Act of 1938 implemented a minimum wage for most occupations and mandated overtime pay for time worked over forty hours per week. In combination, these laws radically changed the relative power of labor with respect to corporate employers. Thus, the number of union members increased from under 10 percent of the labor force in the late 1930s to nearly 30 percent fifteen years later (Council of Economic Advisors, 2015).

In 1936, Congress passed the Robinson–Patman Act to limit price discrimination by prohibiting suppliers from providing goods at lower prices to "preferred customers," such as chain stores. The effect was to protect smaller shopkeepers from being underpriced by national chains such as A&P (the Walmart of its time).

3.3 The Glorious Postwar Years

The final major antitrust legislation was the Celler–Kefauver Anti-Merger Act of 1950. Congress was motivated in part by concerns that monopoly in industry had enabled the rise of fascism in Europe: As Brandeis had pointed out, concentrated economic power can create concentrated political power, to the detriment of democracy.[25] Celler–Kefauver would prevent this with strict limits on how firms could grow through acquisition, including not just horizontal mergers (buying competitors) but also vertical integration (buying suppliers or

---

[24] See Davis and Mizruchi (1999) on the evolution of American commercial banking.

[25] See Crane (2020) on the potential ties between fascism and monopoly in Germany and the United States.

distributors) and even conglomerate mergers (buying firms in unrelated industries). Celler–Kefauver largely completed the arc of American antitrust law and created substantial barriers to horizontal and vertical mergers for the next three decades.

Surprisingly, American companies did not stop growing after 1950. Some grew organically: By 1962, General Motors had a 51 percent share of the US auto market and employed over 600,000 workers (Knoema, 2020). Others conglomerated, nudged by Celler–Kefauver's restrictions. The manufacturing company ITT expanded from 132,000 employees in 1960 to 392,000 in 1970 by buying up hundreds of familiar brands across many industries: home construction, semiconductor manufacturing, life insurance, auto parts, vocational education, Avis car rental, Twinkies and Wonder Bread, Sheraton Hotels, and the Chilean national telephone company. Relative to the size of the economy, conglomerates were simply massive: by 1970, the twenty-five largest American corporations employed the equivalent of 11 percent of the private labor force, a number never equaled before or since. Furthermore, the political power of business had hardly been tamed: ITT was a central player in the 1973 coup against President Salvador Allende in Chile (New York Times, 1972). Big companies could be powerful even without dominating any particular industry.

The wave of conglomerate acquisitions continued for another decade and diversification became a standard tool of corporate growth. By 1980 most major corporations in America were diversified. Ford made cars, trucks, tractors, aerospace equipment, real estate developments, and loans. Westinghouse built nuclear plants, locomotive engines, missile launchers, elevators, office furniture, high school curricula, wristwatches, and Seven Up. And General Electric did it all: jet engines, plastics, X-ray machines, kitchen appliances, televisions, steam turbines, uranium mining, financial services, and light bulbs.

In short, if the aim of postwar antitrust was to prevent the "curse of bigness," it failed miserably. American corporations had become massive, gerrymandered districts on the industrial landscape.

3.4 Bork's Backlash against Antitrust and the Revenge of Big Business

The standard account of the new anti-monopolists describes a happy, competitive postwar American economy full of small family businesses and local shopkeepers engaged in friendly competition to serve their customers better, thanks to antitrust's limits on corporate power. According to Barry Lynn (2020: 21):

America in 1950 was a land of independent farms, independent stores, independent businesses, and independent communities ruled to a very large degree by the people who lived in them. It was a world in which almost any citizen who wanted to get ahead had real opportunity to do so (or, at least, any white male citizen with access to the generous government programs and bank credit of the time).

But this idyllic world reached a turning point in 1978 when Robert Bork, a Yale law professor schooled at the notorious University of Chicago, published *The Paradox of Antitrust.*

According to critics today, Bork shamelessly misrepresented the purpose of the Sherman Act, arguing that the entire point of antitrust was to enhance consumer welfare as measured by the prices customers paid.[26] As Bork saw things, quantifiable metrics wielded by trained economists were essential to proving that monopoly power was harmful. Moreover, corporate power without consumer harm was irrelevant. Big firms generally got big by being better at what they did than competitors, not by underhand tactics. Predatory pricing never happened in the real world. And Bork twisted the meaning of common-sense words. Competition, for instance, becomes "any state of affairs in which consumer welfare cannot be increased by moving to an alternate state of affairs by judicial decree" (Paul, 2020: 416.)

Readers today can evidently see through Bork's tortured reasoning and flimsy evidence, just as we now realize that disco and polyester clothing were a mistake. Tim Wu (2018: 89) quotes Herbert Hoverkamp: "Not a single statement in the legislative history comes close to stating the conclusions that Bork drew." Sally Hubbard (2020: 12) points out that Bork and his disciples claim "the laws' goal first and foremost is to promote corporate efficiency," yet "efficiency" appears nowhere in the text of the Sherman Act. Khan and Vaheesan (2017: 277) assert "the passage of the Sherman Act was animated by at least three goals: (1) the distribution of political economic power, (2) the prevention of unjust wealth transfers from consumers and small suppliers to large entities, and (3) the preservation of open markets," yet Bork narrowed this to just one. But somehow economists, judges, politicians, and regulators were mesmerized by the sophistry of this wild-haired scholar. And once Ronald Reagan was elected to the presidency, the project of antitrust – to protect citizens and democracy from monopoly power – slipped into a coma, as Bork's fellow travelers were injected into our regulatory and judicial apparatus like per- and polyfluoroalkyl substances (PFASs) into the water supply.

---

[26] Paul (2021) provides a rigorous unpacking of the true legislative history of the Sherman Act.

The Antitrust Division of the Justice Department relaxed horizontal merger guidelines in 1982, making it easier for corporations to acquire their competitors, and the FTC followed suit. The standards for judging whether a proposed merger was bad for competition shifted from industry concentration, which is easy for anyone to see, to inscrutable economic mumbo jumbo. The number of government lawyers dedicated to antitrust spiraled downward. And even the election of Democrats to the White House failed to rouse antitrust from its slumber. Four decades later we are heirs to the trauma of Borkism.

The results?

> You probably have a phone made by one of two companies. You likely bank at one of four giant banks, and fly on one of four big airlines. You connect with friends with either Facebook, WhatsApp, or Instagram, all of which are owned by one company. You get your internet through Comcast or AT&T. Data about your thoughts goes into a database owned by Google, what you buy into Amazon or Walmart, and what you owe into Experian or Equifax. You live in a world structured by concentrated corporate power.
>
> (Stoller, 2019: xiv).

3.5 How Monopolists Turned the Twenty-First Century American Economy into a Dystopian Hellscape

How, exactly, do monopolists perpetrate their economic crimes? The standard story is straightforward. Industry concentration (however achieved) leads to monopoly power and less competition. A company with a large market share is able to charge its captives prices that are too high (or, sometimes, too low, or too different), pay lower wages, extort suppliers, and use underhand tactics to compete with actual or potential rivals. Market share also gives firms excessive political power – including undue influence over their regulators.

The Congressional subcommittee report on the monopolistic actions of Big Tech companies is something of a master class in the exercise of monopoly power.[27] Facebook maintains its monopoly power in social networking by buying up nascent competitors before they can grow big enough to be threatening, or shamelessly copying their innovations, all while serving up dangerous misinformation on a global scale. Google's monopoly power in internet search and its vast economies of scale and scope make it indispensable for businesses seeking to share information with consumers, who are forced to buy ads on Google to avoid being invisible. Amazon's dominance in online retail makes it the sole distribution channel for hundreds of thousands of businesses, who have

---

[27] Subcommittee on Antitrust, Commercial and Administrative Law of the Committee on the Judiciary (2020). Hereafter, "subcommittee report."

no realistic alternative to meeting whatever demands Amazon makes of them – even as the company uses its extensive surveillance capabilities to create and market its own copycat goods. And Apple controls the operating system of the most popular smartphone in the United States and the only store iPhone owners can use to download apps, depriving consumers of alternatives and forcing software developers to pay its commissions and meet its arbitrary demands.

This sounds bad if you are a small business or app developer seeking to sell your product over the Internet. But a consumer might well ask: How bad is it really? If I go to Amazon.com and search for cat litter, or headphones, or vitamin D, or hubcaps for a Ford Fusion, I encounter many different brands, and for any brand there are often multiple sellers with surprisingly diverse prices, all ready to ship their products to my home in the coming hours or days. If I want to have a video call with my sister in Scotland, I have my choice of Zoom, Skype, Google Hangouts, Microsoft Teams, FaceTime, WhatsApp, WebEx, and more – all free. If I want to watch "The Princess Bride," I can choose from Hulu, HBO, Amazon Prime, YouTube, and several more obscure outlets. And if I want food to show up at my door from four different restaurants for every member of my family (vegan for me, Thai for my wife, Mexican for my son, pizza for my daughter), I can contact DoorDash, Grubhub, Postmates, or UberEats. Admittedly, I may be forced to wash the meal down with bland beer from a brewery ultimately owned by hated monopolist AB InBev. Or I can choose a hoppy IPA from one of the half-dozen microbrewers within bicycling distance of my home.

It is possible that the biggest victims of our comatose antitrust system are not consumers. It should not be surprising that an antitrust system oriented toward keeping consumer prices low has created an economy in which consumer prices for many goods are, in fact, low. Perhaps the biggest costs of this system are borne elsewhere.

4 The Problems with the Monopoly Narrative

Let's be very clear: Profit-oriented corporations are responsible for a lot of mischief. Indeed, nearly every pathology in American society today was created or exacerbated by corporations.

The opioid epidemic, caused by profit-seeking pharmaceutical corporations, kills more than 60,000 people per year and has single-handedly reduced the average life expectancy of Americans (Salam, 2017). (Overdose deaths rose to nearly 90,000 per year during the COVID-19 pandemic – Goodnough, 2021.) Of American adults, 40 percent are clinically obese largely due to the efforts of corporations that sell fine-tuned formulas of sugar, salt, and fat in efficient calorie-delivery vehicles, packaged in single-use plastic containers that will be on this earth long after our species has become extinct (Richtel and Jacobs, 2018). Vaping companies have introduced a new generation of teens and preteens to the joys of nicotine addiction, advertising their candy-flavored pods on child-oriented websites (Sales, 2020). Social media companies have created safe spaces for plotting sedition and genocide, drawing on the latest behavioral insights to create compulsive usage while undermining the business model of a free press (Lewis, 2017). Ridehailing and delivery companies are funding legislation to destroy the employment relation in America, turning workers into a corps of precarious on-demand contractors (Edelson, 2021). Fossil fuel corporations aggressively hurtle our species toward climate extinction while funding deceptive research that denies their culpability.[28]

If you are looking for corporate wrongdoing in America, you don't have to go far. But the biggest problem is not monopoly – it's shareholder capitalism. We would not be better off by having more profit-seeking competitors selling opioids, overprocessed food, candy-flavored nicotine, addictive social media, gig jobs, or fossil fuels. There are many ways to damage society that do not involve monopoly.

Moreover, the consensus monopoly narrative is rooted in a set of stylized facts and selective evidence that do not hold up to cross-examination. Let's start with the main factual claim of the new anti-monopolists: that after Bork published his notorious tome and Reagan's appointees gutted traditional antitrust enforcement, industries across the board became concentrated. Recent books and articles about the horrors of monopoly often cite a claim that 75 percent of American industries have become more concentrated over the last two decades. And here it is, in the opening sentence of an article in an academic journal: "Since the late 1990s, over 75% of US industries have experienced an increase in concentration levels" – at least through 2014, when the data end.[29] Other sources relying on the same data come to similar conclusions.

This claim is cited verbatim in the second paragraph of the "Fact Sheet" for Biden's executive order on competition[30] and in various ways in many different anti-monopoly tracts:

- "Since the year 2000, across U.S. industries, the Herfindahl – Hirschman index, which measures market concentration, has increased in over 75 percent of industries." Wu (2018: 20)

---

[28] See Oreskes and Conway (2010) on the corruption of science by industry.
[29] Grullon et al. (2019: 697). See also Gutierrez and Phillipon (2017) and De Loecker et al. (2020).
[30] www.whitehouse.gov/briefing-room/statements-releases/2021/07/09/fact-sheet-executive-order-on-promoting-competition-in-the-american-economy/.

- "One study finds that 75 per cent of industries in the US have experienced a reduction in the number of competitors and a corresponding increase in levels of industry concentration in the last two decades." Meagher (2020: 21)
- "Between 1997 and 2014, corporate concentration increased in 80 percent of industries by an average of 90 percent, according to economists." Hubbard (2020: 11)
- "Over the past two decades, 75 percent of industries have seen a significant increase in concentration. Corporate profits are also up, and both concentration and profitability are at levels that existed in the 1970s and before." Konczal (2021: 148)

But wait: The same article that claims 75 percent of industries have become more concentrated since 2000 reports a dramatic *decline* in industry concentration during the three years after the 1982 Department of Justice merger guidelines. The authors state, "Consistent with increased competition documented by prior studies ... the concentration index declines beginning in the 1980s and remains low until the late 1990s, reaching its lowest point in 1996–97."[31] If industries freed from antitrust inevitably become concentrated, then why would industry concentration drop for fifteen straight years after Bork's ideas were put into practice?

The short answer is that evidence of increasing industry concentration is weak, unsystematic, and inconsistent, and does not always tell us very much about the actual state of competition.

4.1 It's Harder Than it Looks to Measure "Market Concentration"

The data behind the widely-cited figure above come from annual sales reported for US-based corporations that are listed on a stock market, with "industry" defined at the 3-digit NAICS level. (Bear with me a moment.) In plain English: for any given year, take all the companies listed on a stock market and incorporated in the US, sort them into their primary industry, add up all the sales for all the companies in the same industry, divide each company's sales by their industry's overall sales, and you get market share data. From there you can calculate various measures of industry concentration – say, how much of the industry's sales come from the four biggest companies, or fancier measures like the Herfindahl-Hirschman Index (the sum of the squared market shares).

An example of a 3-digit NAICS industry is "Leather and allied products manufacturing." As the authors point out in an online appendix,[32] this industry includes Coach (which makes fancy handbags), Nike (which markets a very

---

[31] Grullon et al. (2019: 701).   [32] https://doi.org/10.1093/rof/rfz007

wide array of sporting goods, including sneakers), and Skechers USA (casual shoes). As is immediately evident, many firms in the same 3-digit industry are not really competitors at all, as their products are not plausible substitutes.

But there are several other problems with this approach. As described above, most major corporations in 1980 were diversified, and some operated in dozens of industries, from soda bottling to nuclear plants, or from casinos to the Chilean national phone company. It is highly misleading to allocate ITT's or GE's total revenues to any single industry. (This problem largely went away, as I will describe below, but then came back.)

A second difficulty is that American corporations have been global for generations and have become even more so over time. S&P 500 companies today generate 30–40% of their revenues overseas (Bacani, 2021; Rekenthaler, 2019). This is particularly true of the high-tech success stories whose products (or services, or whatever) are purveyed online. Two-thirds of Netflix subscribers are outside of the US and Canada; 67% of Apple's sales come from outside the US; most of Alphabet's revenues are from overseas. It makes no sense to include foreign revenues in measures of domestic market concentration. Consider an extreme case: Yum Brands (proprietor of Pizza Hut, Taco Bell, and KFC) spun off its China-based outlets into a new company named Yum China Holdings, which operates over 10,000 stores and is the largest restaurant company in China. But because it is incorporated in Delaware and traded on the New York Stock Exchange, Yum China Holdings' revenues would contribute to US industry concentration in NAICS code 722 (Food Services and Drinking Places). Conversely, Anheuser-Busch is now owned by AB InBev of Belgium, and thus a foreign company whose US sales are not captured by this measure.

Moreover, measuring industry concentration at a national level is often irrelevant to how competitive an industry is on the ground.[33] A town with five grocery stores, each with a 20% local market share, has the same degree of competition whether the stores are separate outlets of national chains or each owned by local grocers, and this is true for almost any local provider (restaurants, retailers, gyms, funeral homes, hospitals, churches). Olive Garden's national sales figures have little relevance for competition in my town (which has many fine local Italian restaurants, thank you very much).[34]

---

[33] Berry et al. (2019) describe how the structure-conduct-performance approach was abandoned by industrial organization economists in the late 1980s but seems to have re-emerged, zombie-like, in recent discussions of antitrust.

[34] Shapiro (2018) provides additional detail on the limitations of connecting industry concentration, competition, and profitability. Rossi-Hansberg et al. (2021) report that in many cases market concentration is actually *declining* at the local level even as it increases at the national level, as the entry of national firms in local markets reduces these markets' concentration.

A fourth problem with using these data is that an increasing number of big companies are not listed on the stock market. The number of listed corporations in the US dropped by half from 1997 to 2012 and has not come back. Much of this is due to failures (e.g., the dot-com collapse in 2000 and the financial industry meltdown in 2008); some is due to horizontal mergers (e.g., Pfizer's serial acquisitions of Warner-Lambert, Pharmacia, and Wyeth). But much of it is due to the unprecedented rise of private equity as an alternative to the public market. During the years that Dell (and Hilton, Chrysler, Hospital Corporation of America, Safeway ...) are owned by PE funds, they don't appear in the market share data, thus distorting their industry's measured concentration. Assets under management in private equity grew by $4 trillion in the past decade, as many familiar brands have been taken private (McKinsey & Co, 2021).

Last, how do we measure "market share" in industries in which companies do not charge for their services? Social media, online search, and many other "concentrated" markets do not have any direct revenues from sales to customers – they are funded by advertising and give away their product for free. Measures of market share when there is no actual market can be arbitrary and difficult to compare with revenue-based shares. For example, what is the market share of Wikipedia, or Linux, or Python?

There are other data one can draw on to calculate industry concentration – e.g., the Economic Census (cf. Autor et al., 2020) – but many of the problems I have mentioned apply here as well. As industrial organization economists have long known, you simply can't infer the state of competition in an industry by toting up the national revenues of firms in that industry. Suppose General Motors and Ford decide to spin off their major parts operations into free-standing public companies (as both did in the 1990s). Nothing changes in the level of concentration based on final revenue in the auto industry, but we now have new revenues appearing by magic in the auto parts industries because "internal" suppliers are now "external."[35] You also can't always tell much by adding up the profits that companies declare each year. Between 1997 and 2017, department store chain Macy's reported earning twice as much cumulative profit as Amazon (Nelson and Karajan, 2017). Which firm is the monopolist – Macy's, or Amazon?

An alternative way to get at "bigness" is to forego industry entirely, and simply examine the aggregate concentration of the economy – that is, how much is controlled by, say, the 500 largest corporations. Here again, we do not see reason to believe the narrative of ever-increasing concentration brought about

---

[35] See White (2002) and White and Yang (2020).

by Bork: "Between the early 1980s and the mid 1990s there was a decline in aggregate concentration as shown by the annual employment percentages and profit percentages of the 500 largest firms in the U.S. economy. Since the mid 1990s, there appear to have been modest increases in both percentages; but those percentages do not seem to have regained the levels of the early 1980s" (White and Yang, 2020: 499). In other words, by some measures, the American economy has never regained the level of concentration it had the year that Reagan was elected.

4.2 There Really Are Some Monopolies Out There, but Our Bigger Problem Is Shareholder Capitalism

If you have a narrative in mind – monopolists are dominating more and more industries! – you will surely be able to find evidence consistent with that narrative. (This is known as the "confirmation bias" in psychology: Once you learn about it, you will see it everywhere.[36]) There are a lot fewer airlines than there used to be (and those that remain do not cycle through bankruptcy quite as often as US Air did). National retail chains have acquired or driven out regional chains – Dayton of Minneapolis, Hudson of Detroit, Marshall Field of Chicago, Federated of Cincinnati, and many other regional chains are all now part of profit-gusher Macy's.[37] The biggest beer companies in America really are big. And since the financial crisis in 2008 the four biggest commercial banks have increased their market share – we are now down to only 5,000 commercial banks in the United States, compared to 12,000 forty years ago.

Some monopolies really do pose hazards to society's well-being. Agriculture, in particular, is made precarious by its hourglass industry structure.[38] But the problem with anecdotage is that it is equally possible to dig up alternative anecdotes that show the opposite. How many different flat-screen television brands are there today? Or video streaming services? Or vegan meat alternatives? Or yoga apps? Or microbrews? Amazon has 1.9 million active sellers, and 140,000 of them generate over $100,000 in annual revenues (Arishekar, 2021). Apple's app store lists two million apps; Google Play lists almost three million. We may not have as many Main Street shopkeepers as we did in that magical year, 1950, but we have a lot more app developers, online merchants, and TikTok influencers.

---

[36] This joke is attributable to Jon Ronson.
[37] Hsieh and Rossi-Hansberg (2019) describe how ICTs have increased economies of scale in retail and other service industries, encouraging consolidation in retail. Of course, competition in on-site retail is highly localized.
[38] The antitrust critique of agriculture, however, often relies on distorted evidence that overstates the dire situation of farmers. See Rosenberg and Stucki (2021).

The new anti-monopolists overlook the more consequential shift that happened after Bork: the rise of shareholder primacy and its focus on share price above all else. The corporate search for monopoly power, for industry segments with "moats" to protect against competition, is a vehicle used toward the ultimate goal of profits for shareholders. Monopoly power is just one tool among many used to serve this end, and as long as shareholder value is the motivating force in our corporate economy, we will not make progress toward a more humane and democratic society.

In the decade prior to Bork's infamous book, economists published a series of provocative works that undermined the postwar corporate détente that underwrote America's brief period of rapid economic growth, increased opportunity, and declining income inequality (ca. 1945–73). Some of these works are well known. Fifty years ago Milton Friedman famously argued in the *New York Times Magazine* that corporations exist to make profits, not to serve higher social purposes – a claim that was considered shocking at the time, yet self-evident today. Alchian and Demsetz (1972: 777) asserted that there was nothing sacred about the boundary between the inside and the outside of a company, and that the contractual relation between a boss and an employee involves no more "authority" than the relation between a customer and a grocer:

> To speak of managing, directing, or assigning workers to various tasks is a deceptive way of noting that the employer continually is involved in renegotiation of contracts on terms that must be acceptable to both parties. Telling an employee to type this letter rather than to file that document is like telling a grocer to sell me this brand of tuna rather than that brand of bread. Alchian and Demsetz (1972: 777)

(This description is notably similar to the minute-by-minute "negotiations" that Uber drivers experience – see Cameron, 2021.) Jensen and Meckling (1976) combined these two elements, describing the corporation as a mere nexus-of-contracts with no tangible social reality. According to this account, the main problem the corporation had to solve was motivating the people who ran it to create shareholder value. If the corporation failed at this task, it was up to outsiders to buy up the company's shares, fire its top managers, and replace them with people more devoted to the company's share price – a process known as the "market for corporate control."

Why would economists say these strange things? Why would they deny the tangible reality of a General Motors or an AT&T, century-spanning institutions that employed hundreds of thousands of Americans, often for a lifetime, and then funded their pensions and health care until death?

The intellectual turn toward neoliberalism, and the invasion of law schools by economists, has received much attention elsewhere. But the impacts of this shift – seeing the corporation as a mere legal fiction that existed to create shareholder value above all else – were profound.[39] These arguments laid the groundwork for the deconstruction of the corporation as a social institution. It created the intellectual underpinning for what happened next, and paved the way for our ephemeral ICT-enabled economy today.

4.3 The Bust-Up Takeover Boom

Reagan's biggest impact on the corporate world was to enable a wave of bust-up takeovers that took apart the massive conglomerates built in the prior generation; this left the economy notably less concentrated than when he started. When Reagan took office in 1981, the modal big American corporation was some variant of a conglomerate, operating in several largely unrelated industries. Autor et al. (2020: 663) report that in 1982 the largest firm in each industry operated in thirteen other industries. In short, General Electric, ITT, and Westinghouse were not outliers, but the norm.

While these companies may have been big, they were not successful – at least as far as the stock market was concerned. (General Electric was the exception, at least for a time.) On average, the more industries a corporation operated in, the more it was undervalued (that is, the price of its shares was lower than it should have been). This was a problem with a solution, at least in principle. Imagine buying ITT and splitting it up into twenty smaller companies: Sheraton hotels, Hartford insurance, Avis rent-a-car, Hostess baked goods, ITT vocational training, and so on. According to the stock market, the whole was worth less than the sum of the parts – and this did not just apply to ITT, but broad swaths of corporate America. By the market's evaluation, the last twenty years of Celler–Kefauver-driven conglomeration had been a giant, tragic mistake.

Meanwhile, financial technologies (including the mundane spreadsheet) were making it easier to value these things and figure out just how much money could be made by buying companies and splitting them up. New methods of funding such as junk bonds and large-scale bridge loans were becoming available. And legal and regulatory changes were making it possible to buy companies from shareholders without getting the permission of the company's managers or board of directors, known as a hostile takeover. (This was done by a "tender offer," which sounds like the title of an Elvis song, but is not as sweet and gentle as it sounds.)

---

[39] I trace this tale in Davis (2009).

All the conditions were in place for the biggest wave of hostile takeovers ever seen. Between 1980 and 1990, 29 percent of listed companies in the Fortune 500 were subject to a tender offer. Most of these were hostile (that is, fought by the company's incumbent board), and they were overwhelmingly successful. In the course of a decade, between hostile takeovers and negotiated mergers, one in three of the largest American corporations changed hands, and the people who ran them were tossed out (albeit often with a tasty severance package).[40]

Unlike prior merger waves, these deals did not result in even larger and more diversified corporations. Instead, the typical deal led to conglomerates being busted up into their component parts and spun off into free-standing companies or sold to related acquirers. The companies that remained received the message, forswearing acquisitions and splitting themselves up into more focused components to escape the fate of their hapless peers. Within a decade, most members of the Fortune 500 were lean, mean, and laser-focused on a core industry competence.[41]

The notion that Reagan's Bork-inflected vision was a gift to Big Business would surely come as a surprise to the one in three CEOs who lost their jobs in the 1980s takeover wave. We tend to remember Gordon Gecko making his "Greed is good" speech but forget the two dozen uncomfortable directors and executives sitting on the stage who had to listen to it and contemplate their impending unemployment. Antitrust did play a part in the takeover wave. Henry Manne (1965) argued that strict antitrust kept badly run companies in business because the most obvious candidates to buy them and fix them – their competitors – were not allowed to do so. Thus, the 1982 horizontal merger guidelines provided some willing customers for busted-out divisions of conglomerates. But this did not yield notably more concentrated industries.

The biggest impact of the Reagan years was to establish that corporations existed first and foremost to create shareholder value, and everything else was secondary. The corporation had been financialized. A way to visualize this is to visit once again the Dow Jones index, this time for 1982 (see Table 3). Note that twenty-two of the thirty Dow companies had been there for half a century or more, and all of them were venerable pillars of American capitalism.

Today, only five are left: Chevron, IBM, Merck, 3M (formerly Minnesota Mining and Manufacturing Company), and Procter & Gamble. Not all the rest have vanished, but many have passed through bankruptcy or are in precarious shape. It is like seeing what's left of your high school football team at your forty-year class reunion. Whatever happened to Bethlehem Steel, or Eastman Kodak, or Westinghouse? Didn't Johns Manville get in trouble with some

---

[40] This is documented in detail in Davis and Stout (1992)

[41] See Davis, Diekmann, and Tinsley (1994) for details on deconglomeration and its impact on corporate size and diversification.

Table 3 The Dow Jones index, 1982

Allied Chemical	General Foods	Owens-Illinois
ALCOA	General Motors	Procter & Gamble
American Can	Goodyear	Sears Roebuck
American Tobacco	IBM	Standard Oil CA (Chevron)
AT&T	International Harvester	Texaco
Bethlehem Steel	International Nickel	Union Carbide
DuPont	International Paper	United Technologies
Eastman Kodak	Johns Manville	US Steel
Exxon	Merck	Westinghouse
General Electric	Minnesota Mining and Manufacturing	Woolworth

asbestos? Is Sears still alive? General Electric was the quarterback, but now it's looking a little ... haggard.

And contrary to the narrative of Borkism, industry consolidation does not account for most of the changes in these companies. They did not go off on a wild frenzy of industry consolidation. Instead, they mostly drifted into irrelevance from which their large initial size was no protection.[42]

4.4 The Outsourcing Wave of the 1990s

The Bork monopoly narrative has a hard time explaining the massive industry restructuring of the 1980s. It also provides little insight into the wave of layoffs and outsourcing that took hold in the 1990s. If companies love getting bigger, then why were so many of them disposing of employees, spinning off divisions, and hiring outside vendors for many of the things they used to do for themselves, like payroll, IT, or even manufacturing? Why would Ford spin off Visteon, its massive parts division, and Associates, its finance group? Why would General Motors spin off Delphi (its own parts division) and Electronic Data Systems, and sell off its finance and electronics businesses? Why would Sara Lee sell off its factories and later spin off its varied brands (Coach, Champion, Hanes), winding up a stub of its former glory?

The short answer is Nikefication. Nike had shown that it was entirely possible to focus on design, branding, and advertising, and to hire overseas contractors to

---

[42] For a detailed industry-level analysis of US public corporations after 2000, see Davis (2017).

do the more labor-intensive work of making sneakers. As the 1990s wore on it became clear that this same model applied in lots of industries, from electronics to pharmaceuticals to pet food. The Internet allowed companies to share design specifications and keep track of dispersed production in real time, and the growth of a set of generic manufacturers allowed them to outsource activities formerly considered essential. Pressured by Wall Street investors, corporations increasingly shrank down to a core and outsourced the rest. Many "original equipment manufacturers" no longer manufactured anything with their name on it. They increasingly looked like the nexus-of-contracts foretold by 1970s-era economists.

Spin-offs and split-ups continue to be rampant across the corporate landscape. In recent years Hewlett-Packard split into two separate companies (products and services), as did Xerox; Time Warner divided into several parts; General Electric spun off almost all its most recognizable divisions, including its massive finance operations, and in late 2021 announced plans for a final split into three free-standing companies; pharma giant Abbott Labs spun off Abbvie; Verizon bought and then sold Yahoo and AOL; AT&T bought and then sold TimeWarner; and so on. Counting up mergers without also counting up demergers yields a deceptive impression that corporations inevitably tend toward gigantism, but in a world driven to outsourcing by relentless demands to increase shareholder value, size is not the most relevant metric of corporate success.

We may have a monopoly problem, but shareholder capitalism is a bigger problem. Trying to fix the pathologies of shareholder capitalism using the tools of antitrust is like trying to make ice hockey safer by changing the color of the puck.

Conceptually, we have an even bigger problem. Software is eating the world, and for dessert it is dining on the categories we have long used to understand the economy. The basic categories we once used to diagnose conditions like "monopoly" have shifted. If "monopoly" is when an American industry is dominated by one or two big corporations, then what happens if "American," "industry," and "big" no longer apply? It is like returning to Paris after Baron Haussmann completely redesigned the central city and trying to locate the family home. Nationality, industry, and size are increasingly misleading categories for understanding our economy. In Sections 5, 6 and 7, we consider each of these.

5 What Is Nationality Now?

What is the nationality of Royal Caribbean Group? The vacation cruise company, which took $11 billion in revenues the year before the COVID-19 pandemic, is headquartered in Miami (so, Caribbean-adjacent), and listed on the New York Stock Exchange. A plurality of its customers come from the United States. But it is not an American company. Its ships fly the flags of many lands, but not the United States – because the globally sourced crew could then be subject to American labor laws.

In fact, Royal Caribbean is incorporated under the laws of Liberia, a country that its executives almost certainly could not locate on an unmarked map of West Africa. The tax benefits are just too attractive to pass up. In the poetic words of RCL's annual report, "We believe that most of our income ... is derived from or incidental to the international operation of a ship or ships and, therefore, is exempt from taxation under Section 883."[43] Like a church or a soup kitchen, Royal Caribbean does not pay US income taxes.

Royal Caribbean is not alone in its ambiguous citizenship. Carnival is incorporated in Panama, while Miami-based Norwegian Cruise Line is, of course, incorporated in ... Bermuda (Kosciolek, 2021). Corporations do not carry a passport, and their nationality is often unclear. Fiat Chrysler, which combined Italian and American automakers, was legally Dutch, and after merging with France's PSA Group (Peugeot, Citroën) to form Stellantis, remained incorporated in the Netherlands. Consulting giant Accenture was Bermudan but is now Irish. And Yum China Holdings, owner of several thousand KFCs and Pizza Huts in China and employing nearly a half-million workers, is incorporated in Delaware and traded on the New York Stock Exchange, making it all-American. Particularly for online businesses (which increasingly encompasses most businesses), nationality is a conundrum.

5.1 Law as a Virtual Product

For the average person, the law is a set of external constraints on their behavior, like the Ten Commandments, handed down through an obscure and vaguely intimidating process and enforced by the police. For a corporation, however, law is an operating system for governing business contracts. As with their other software purchases, corporations are discriminating consumers when they shop for law. They are able to fine-tune where they choose to incorporate, where they stash their copyrights and trademarks, what arbitrator will settle their commercial or labor disputes, even where they will sue their rivals – regardless of the physical location of their work (if any). Courts may reside in a particular place, but law does not.

---

[43] United States Securities and Exchange Commission, www.sec.gov/ix?doc=/Archives/edgar/data/884887/000088488721000006/rcl-20201231.htm.

If law is a product, then who are the vendors? Who competes to attract customers, and how? In the United States, corporate law is made by each of the fifty states, and for some the fees for administering corporate law are a big business. Tiny Delaware is the legal home of over two-thirds of the Fortune 500 companies and receives a substantial part of its annual budget from corporate licensing fees.[44] Thanks to revenues from its corporate customers, Delaware can offer low property taxes and no sales tax to its citizens. Delaware is the McDonald's of corporate law, fast, clean, and predictable – all of which make it an attractive legal domicile for a large majority of American corporations.

When the physical location of a company's activities is unrelated to its place of incorporation, there is little need to be provincial. Since the end of World War II, Liberia has provided "flags of convenience" for merchant ships as well as incorporation services for companies such as Royal Caribbean. There are many advantages to Liberian incorporation, notably when it comes to taxes. Information about how to incorporate can be found online at www.liscr.com /liberian-corporate-registry. And to highlight the fact that law is a business service – like IT, accounting, and payroll processing – Liberia's ship and corporate registry has been outsourced to a corporate vendor housed near Dulles Airport in Virginia. (Presumably shareholder suits still would be litigated in Monrovia.)

Offshore incorporation is not just for tax cheats.[45] Today, even legitimate businesses have legitimate reasons to incorporate in Bermuda, a legitimate country. When Accenture went public as a Bermuda corporation, its rationale was plain enough: We are a global company operating in dozens of countries around the world, with no central headquarters. Why should our citizenship be tied to any single city or country? And when the Obama administration hinted that it was skeptical of Accenture's Bermuda-based operations, it quickly reincorporated in Ireland, an even more legitimate island nation (Drucker, 2009). As Martin Wolf (2004) put it, today's corporations are rootless cosmopolitans, with at best sentimental ties to any physical territory.

If Accenture – née Arthur Andersen Consulting of Chicago – can claim to be placeless with a straight face, why would we expect tech companies to be rooted in any particular locale? Accenture is half a million strong, and its teams of employees work in tangible, physical offices. When Coinbase went public in

---

[44] See Urban Institute (2021).

[45] Or, if not tax cheats per se, tax avoiders. *The Guardian* reported in June 2021 that, "An Irish subsidiary of Microsoft made a profit of $315bn (£222bn) last year but paid no corporation tax, as it is 'resident' for tax purposes in Bermuda. The company, Microsoft Round Island One, posted profits last year equal to nearly three-quarters of Ireland's entire gross domestic product (GDP) – despite having zero employees" (Neate, 2021).

April 2021, on the other hand, its prospectus listed no address, and noted that it was a remote-first company with no physical headquarters.[46] Instead, most of its 1,249 employees worked wherever. As with dozens of tech companies after the COVID-19 pandemic struck, most of the Coinbase labor force works from home.

"Work-from-home" is almost certain to mean that employees who live in the vicinity of a company's remaining facilities will face competition from contractors who may live anywhere in the world. (For those concerned about employer monopsony power: yay?) Companies have already become practiced at managing outsourced workers in India and the Philippines, and it will not be much of a stretch to accommodate a few more. The placeless enterprise staffed by remote contractors is certain to be increasingly common. Inevitably, as a Silicon Valley informant told me, some work-from-home tech employees are now trying to claim a home address in a tax-free domicile far from high-tax California. Cash-strapped tax authorities may have little reason to track down scofflaws claiming to live in Texas or Luxembourg . . . or Liberia.

5.2 On the Internet, Nobody Knows If You're Really Estonian

Because law is a business service operating in a competitive industry, it was inevitable that an online-first provider would emerge to take on the brick-and-mortar incumbents, as Amazon.com took on Borders and Barnes & Noble.

The first entrant in this new category was Estonia with its e-Residency program, launched in 2014. E-Residency is aimed primarily at internet entrepreneurs, providing access to Estonia's online incorporation, payment, and banking services. Notably, e-Residency does not entail citizenship in real-world Estonia and does not give e-Residents the right to live in Estonia. Like the corporation, it is a legal fiction useful for business purposes. According to its website,[47] "E-Residency allows digital entrepreneurs to manage business from anywhere, entirely online." At the time of writing, there are over 80,000 e--Residents[48] from over 160 countries who have started more than 10,000 businesses (Vatte, 2019).

e-Estonia is not a tax haven or a Master of Fine Arts conceptual art project by an ironic hipster art student. Rather, it is a recognition of the inevitable evolution of business law in an online-first economy. We can expect to see more entrants into the crypto-nationality business.

---

[46] United States Securities and Exchange Commission, www.sec.gov/Archives/edgar/data/1679788/000162828021003168/coinbaseglobalincs-1.htm.
[47] See RSH Technologies (2021).   [48] https://e-resident.gov.ee/dashboard/.

Note that even online-first enterprises cannot always escape entanglements with corporeal court systems. Facebook's terms of service are very clear about where any complaints will be litigated: "For any claim, cause of action, or dispute you have against us that arises out of or relates to these Terms or the Facebook Products ('claim'), you agree that it will be resolved exclusively in the U.S. District Court for the Northern District of California or a state court located in San Mateo County" (Facebook, 2021). But if it's a dispute within Facebook (e.g., "Should former President Trump be permanently banned from the Facebook platform?"), the company will turn to its own internal supreme court (Ovide, 2021).

As Facebook demonstrates, being a sovereign state is not essential to operating a system of laws and their adjudication. Some of the more novel new online industries have created their own court systems to resolve disputes, like the admiralty courts of old. "Ransomware-as-a-Service" (RaaS) vendor DarkSide, which provides tools for hackers to seize control of the data of victims and collects a fee based on the size of the ransom paid to their affiliates, relies on escrow deposits and a third-party virtual court system operating on the Dark Web to ensure that there is honor among thieves (and extortionists). Trials are semi-public, which creates incentives for honest dealing (Bracken, 2021).

It is not hard to visualize virtual laws and virtual courts for virtual commerce, and as globally dispersed transactions for both capital and labor increasingly take place online, a global standard may emerge for the governance of boundaryless exchange.

5.3 The Market Share for Placeless Businesses

In the past year I have given talks in San Francisco, Singapore, Vancouver, Melbourne, London, Palo Alto, Cambridge (Massachusetts), Cambridge (UK), Washington, Copenhagen, Denver, Milwaukee, Utrecht, Manchester, Oxford, and State College, Pennsylvania, among other places – all without leaving home. (At the time of writing, it has been sixteen months since I last took a flight.)

During the same period my good friend from high school, Patrick Olson, recorded an album at his home in California that received a highly enthusiastic reception on Spotify. He is a very talented songwriter, but during the COVID-19 pandemic, playing with a live band in a studio was out of the question. Of course, anyone with a Macintosh computer has a built-in music studio already, and Patrick discovered that you can commission high-end studio musicians to record parts of your songs from wherever they happen to be. His method is to ask for three different takes – standard, lively, and "how you wish it had been written" – then combine the instruments bar by bar in his virtual home studio to create the finished track. Voilà: a tight band composed of musicians who have never been in the same state together.[49]

Activities that we imagined required being in the same place – leading a seminar discussion, playing with a band, collaborating on software – can be done by geographically dispersed groups, and the COVID-19 pandemic has demonstrated that diverse enterprises can thrive after the office goes dark. For many forms of collaboration, geography has become largely irrelevant.

The increasing placelessness of the corporation makes market power a conundrum. For virtual products accessed via the Internet and potentially originating anywhere, how do we contemplate market share? Take Spotify, the popular music streaming app. It is based in Sweden, incorporated in Luxembourg, and traded on the New York Stock Exchange, but its service is available around the world. Are its potential competitors "all music available over the Web"? Or TikTok, the wildly popular short-form video app, which may or may not compete with Facebook, Instagram, Snapchat, YouTube, and others. Its Chinese owner, ByteDance, scrupulously segregates the Chinese and US variants of the app, hosting them on servers in their own geographic market (Broderick, 2019). Nonetheless, in August 2020 President Trump threatened to shut down TikTok unless it was sold to a "very American" company like Microsoft, a threat that ultimately proved hollow (Robertson, 2020). Or Grindr, the popular gay dating app. In 2016 Beijing Kunlun Tech Co., based in China, bought Grindr. Three years later the Committee on Foreign Investment in the United States forced the company to sell the app, citing national security concerns (Dean, 2020). Does Grindr compete with all means of meeting up, or all online dating services (Match.com, Eharmony), or only those with smartphone apps (Tinder, Bumble), or only those targeting a gay audience? And how, if at all, does its purported nationality matter for its market power?

In a corporate world of legal masala and industrial mashups, assessing market power will be an ongoing source of confusion. And when the Great Pacific Garbage Patch is declared a libertarian crypto-state, what will its currency be?

6 What Is Industry Now?

What industry does Coinbase operate in? According to the prospectus it issued before going public in April 2021, "you could think of our products as a safe and easy-to-use platform to buy, sell, store, save, spend, and use cryptocurrency . . .

---

[49] Patrick's magical music can be enjoyed at https://open.spotify.com/artist/ 1wUPEoJgkMBv0NzZSWfOnZ.

People are using cryptoccurrency to earn, spend, save, stake, borrow, lend, vote, and perform many other types of economic activity."[50]

Imagine explaining this business to yourself circa 2008, before Bitcoin emerged. "It's like a brokerage, but for current and future currencies that exist outside the realm of nation-states, 'mined' by solving math problems, housed in the cloud on an anonymous nonfungible ledger that exists in dispersed databases ... oh, forget it, just come back in fifteen years." Now try explaining to your younger self how a "crypto exchange" could be valued at $85 billion on its first day of trading, when Goldman Sachs – the most venerable and prestigious Wall Street bank – was worth $110 billion.

When forced to declare its industry using the traditional Standard Industrial Classification (SIC) system, Coinbase defaulted to 7389 – "Business services, not elsewhere classified." This turns out to be a crowded space: food delivery service DoorDash, whose stated mission is "[t]o grow and empower local economies," also claimed this industry, as did Lyft, whose mission is to "[i]mprove people's lives with the world's best transportation."

Industry rivals Coinbase, DoorDash, and Lyft all face the same problem. Our system of industrial classification is not equipped for the boundary issues raised by software eating the world. The "technology industry" is not an industry, and this raises real challenges when it comes to assessing basic descriptive facts such as industry concentration.

6.1 Industry Boundaries After Software Has Eaten the World

In 2020 and 2021, several technology companies made their debut on the stock market. Airbnb provides a platform to rent lodgings on a short-term basis. Is it in the hotel industry? Coursera gives learners access to courses online. Olo is an "on-demand commerce platform for multi-location restaurant brands." Asana is "a work management platform that helps teams orchestrate work, from daily tasks to cross-functional strategic initiatives." Palantir builds "software platforms for large institutions whose work is essential to our way of life," particularly in intelligence and defense. Bentley Systems' "software solutions are used to design, engineer, build and operate large constructed assets such as roadways, bridges, buildings, industrial and power plants and utility network." C3.ai provides "applications that enable the rapid deployment of enterprise-scale AI applications of extraordinary scale and complexity that offer significant social and economic benefit." Snowflake is "pioneering the Data Cloud, an ecosystem

---

[50] United States Securities and Exchange Commission,
     www.sec.gov/Archives/edgar/data/1679788/000162828021003168/coinbaseglobalincs-1
     .htm.

where Snowflake customers, partners, and data providers can break down data silos and derive value from rapidly growing data sets in secure, governed, and compliant ways."[51]

This is a rich and diverse buffet of tech nerditude that spans hotels, restaurants, schools, highways, infrastructure construction, spying, and, apparently, clouds. And yet all these businesses are classified in SIC code 7372 ("Prepackaged software"). By tradition, this means we should regard them as competitors. Uber also classified itself as 7372, while its most obvious direct competitor, Lyft, went with 7389. (Note to researchers: Good luck trying to use revenues or – God forbid – profits to figure out industry concentration for "Prepackaged software.")

It should be clear that our traditional methods of classifying companies into industries have not kept up. And if industry boundaries are relatively arbitrary, then how should we think about industry concentration and monopoly power?

6.2 Markets, Industries, Competition

Commonly used terms can take on specialized definitions, and so it is in the world of markets, industries, and monopoly. A *product market* is a set of products that buyers regard as substitutes for each other. For the right price, buyers are willing to switch from one offering to another.

Market definition – identifying products that are substitutable – is essential to understanding competition and monopoly power. Unsurprisingly, market definition is contentious. A company being sued for antitrust violations might want to define its market as broadly as possible ("We're in the nutrition industry," or "We help people get from one place to another"), while its opponents might go for a more fine-grained definition ("The market for fiber-optic broadband in Duluth, Minnesota" or "The market for lemonade on the 700 block of Maple Street"). Louis Kaplow of Harvard Law School describes market definition as "impossible and counterproductive." It is tricky in markets for homogeneous

---

[51] Prospectuses are available as follows:

Airbnb: www.sec.gov/Archives/edgar/data/1559720/000119312520294801/d81668ds1.htm;
Coursera: www.sec.gov/Archives/edgar/data/1651562/000119312521071525/d65490ds1.htm;
Olo: www.sec.gov/Archives/edgar/data/1431695/000119312521049073/d867519ds1.htm;
Asana: www.sec.gov/Archives/edgar/data/1477720/000119312520228462/d855753ds1.htm;
Palantir: www.sec.gov/Archives/edgar/data/1321655/000119312520230013/d904406ds1.htm;
Bentley Systems: www.sec.gov/Archives/edgar/data/1031308/000155837020010811/bsy-20200821xs1.htm;
C3.ai: www.sec.gov/Archives/edgar/data/1577526/000162828020016443/c3ais-1.htm;
Snowflake: www.sec.gov/Archives/edgar/data/1640147/000162828020013010/snowflakes-1.htm.

goods with a national scope (perhaps sugar, lead, or copper) and impossible for others. Of course, not everyone agrees with Professor Kaplow, and there is a large literature and a lucrative side-hustle for economists in market definition.[52]

We do not need to resolve any controversies about market definition – that's what antitrust lawyers and industrial organization economists are for. But even *industry definition* is complicated, leaving aside issues of the relevant geography and questions of substitutability.

Industries are groups of companies that produce the same goods or services, or produce things in the same way. There is already an ambiguity here: In the first definition, "industry," in the eyes of the consumer, is based on the products that companies sell. But, with respect to the second definition, the widely used SIC system, last updated in 1987, and the more recent North American Industry Classification System (NAICS) both classify establishments based on their production processes, not their outputs.[53] In the first case, industry is about *what*; in the second, it is about *how*.

If you visit many workplaces today you will see rooms full of people staring at screens and typing on keyboards, occasionally talking on the phone, with breaks now and then to head to conference rooms to talk to other people. (This seems to describe most of what happens at a university, for instance.) Based on their "production process," they may indeed be in the same industry. But the production process may not tell us that much about the *business model* – how the company makes money – which would seem essential for understanding its industry.

Consider the industries represented in the 1912 Dow Jones index: sugar, rubber, leather, lead, copper, steel. Each of these industries had existed for generations, and they still exist today. It is easy enough to visualize what the products are, to calculate market shares, and to conceive how a single producer or a cartel might come to dominate the American steel or sugar market. The business model in these industries was not especially complicated, nor were potential competitive strategies for industry participants. You could implement cost-saving technologies through mass production and mass distribution. If there were economies of scale, that meant that bigger firms could offer lower prices and would come to dominate the industry. Or you might use sleazier tactics of the sort contemplated by the Sherman and Clayton Acts: forming

---

[52] See Kaplow (2013) and Werden (2014).

[53] "NAICS will be erected on a production-oriented, or supply-based, conceptual framework. This means that producing units that use identical or similar production processes will be grouped together in NAICS"; www.naics.com/history-naics-code/.

cartels to fix prices, buying key suppliers to cut out competitors, tying sales to purchases of other products you produced.

But business models evolved substantially after the Clayton Act, as industry became more differentiated. Sugar companies earned their revenues directly, by selling sugar. Broadcast networks, on the other hand, made money by selling advertising. Their business model entails attracting attention with their visible product (programming) and selling that attention to advertisers. The business models of Facebook and Google Search descend from this approach.

Many tech companies today have business models that are utterly inscrutable as a byproduct of software eating the world. This can make it difficult to assign them to a fixed industry category, based on either product or process. Uber clearly creates competition for taxi companies, but it claims it is a digital marketplace company, not a transportation company – so much so that it professes to consider drivers incidental to its business operations. After California's legislature passed a bill aimed at classifying some gig workers as employees, Uber's chief legal counsel stated: "Several previous rulings have found that drivers' work is outside the usual course of Uber's business, which is serving as a technology platform for several different types of digital market-places" (Hawkins, 2019). This did not prevent Uber from contributing tens of millions of dollars to support California's Proposition 22, which definitively classified Uber drivers as contractors. It is almost as if René Magritte were drawing the industry boundaries: "This is not a transportation company."

Facebook and Google say they are not media companies, even though much of the population accesses media through their platforms – nor are they advertising companies, even though nearly all their revenues come from advertising. Google listed "Information Retrieval Systems" in its initial public offering (IPO) prospectus; Facebook asserted it was in "Computer and Data Processing Systems." And Snapchat claims in its prospectus to be a camera company – an industry in which they surely have a dominant market share, since Snap's 2020 revenues were double the total sales of digital cameras in the United States.[54] Meanwhile, the trading platform Robinhood, which gained infamy as the cradle of meme-stock bubbles in early 2021, makes money not through charging its retail "customers" fees for executing trades (a service it offers for free) but by "payment for order flow" – fees paid by market-makers for routing trades to them. In a sense, it is the Facebook of finance. (For the purpose of its IPO, Robinhood defaulted to 7372, "Prepackaged software."[55])

---

[54] Snap's prospectus is at www.sec.gov/Archives/edgar/data/1564408/000119312517029199/
d270216ds1.htm; see Statista (2021) for revenues for the actual camera industry.

[55] www.sec.gov/Archives/edgar/data/1783879/000162828021013318/robinhoods-1.htm.

Categorizing companies into industries based on process helps explain why enterprises selling very different services to very different customers can end up being lumped into the same industry. After all, much of their process involves people staring at screens and typing on keyboards.

Industry categories based on *process* may not be very informative after software has eaten the world. How about categories based on *products*? Recent advances in computational methods have allowed some intriguing innovations here. Public corporations in the United States are required to give accurate and up-to-date descriptions of the major products they offer in annual reports filed with the SEC. In an ingenious approach, Hoberg and Phillips (2016) use the nouns in the "Description of business" section of these reports to track the extent to which companies overlap in how they describe their products, reasoning that the more words they have in common, the closer they are as competitors. (It is slightly more complex than that, but let's forego a discussion of cosine similarity for now.) Using this approach, all pairs of firms can be mapped relative to each other, with industries defined by "neighborhoods" of companies with greater overlap. As companies change the description of their product mix over time, they can move around on the map so that the boundaries of industries can shift like cloud formations. These are "textual network industry classifications" (TNICs). TNICs yield a quite different industry mapping than the SIC or NAICS, which should give us real pause for thought when it comes to claims about industries inevitably becoming more concentrated – especially since one of the most common tactics used by firms with close competitors in their neighborhood is to differentiate their products from those of their competitors and head toward a different neighborhood.

This approach, based on products and not process, comes much closer to capturing what critics have in mind when they refer to concentrated industries. Put another way, it illuminates just how little we understand trends in industry concentration, since the "industry" construct is so malleable and changes so much over time.

6.3 Antitrust and the Technology Meta-Industry

The Congressional subcommittee report on antitrust in 2020 sought to avoid pedantic discussions of industry by essentially creating its own system for describing the new technology firms.[56] The ten major product markets identified are:

- Online search ("Online search engines enable users to retrieve webpages and information stored on the Internet").

---

[56] See Subcommittee on Antitrust, Commercial and Administrative Law of the Committee on the Judiciary (2020: Section IV, pp. 77–132).

- Online commerce ("Online commerce, also known as e-commerce, is the activity of buying or selling products or services using the Internet").
- Social networks and social media ("Social media products and services include social networking, messaging, and media platforms designed to engage people by facilitating sharing, creating, and communicating content and information online").
- Mobile app stores ("Mobile application stores [app stores] are digital stores that enable software developers to distribute software applications [apps] to mobile device users").
- Mobile operating systems ("A mobile operating system [OS] provides a mobile device with its underlying functionality, such as user interface, motion commands, button controls, and facilitates the operation of the device's features, such as the microphone, camera, and GPS").
- Digital mapping ("Digital mapping provides users with virtual maps of the physical world").
- Cloud computing ("Cloud computing refers to the service that enables remote storage and software programs on demand through the Internet"; segments include software as a service; platform as a service; and infrastructure as a service).
- Voice assistant ("Voice assistants act as a user interface that enables exchanges between computing devices through a person's voice").
- Web browsers ("A web browser is software that retrieves and displays from the Internet").
- Digital advertising ("There are two principal form [sic] of digital advertising: search advertising and display advertising. Search advertising refers to digital ads on desktop or mobile search engines, such as the Google.com homepage, displayed via 'search ad tech' alongside search engine result … Display advertising refers to the delivery of digital ad content to ad space on websites and mobile apps, which is referred to as 'inventory'.").

Some of these products are old (commercial web browsers date back to the launch of Netscape in 1994); others are far more recent (e.g., voice assistants). All are domains in which companies compete aggressively. Whether they count as "industries" or "markets" is another matter.

The Congressional subcommittee report is structured around an analysis of the brutal competitive tactics used by four tech companies: Facebook, Google/ Alphabet, Amazon, and Apple. Each is regarded as a monopolist in one or two domains: Facebook for social networking, Google for online search and search advertising, Amazon for online retail, and Apple for mobile operating systems. But what is notable is that all of them operate (or have operated) in many of these categories at once. Facebook competes in social networking/social media and advertising. Apple has a mobile operating system, an app store, a voice assistant, digital mapping, and a web browser. Google has maps, search, operating systems, an app store, a web browser, voice assistant, cloud computing, and advertising. Amazon has online retail, cloud computing, voice assistant, and advertising. All of them enter and sometimes exit new markets on an almost daily basis – it is fair to assume that all will offer products in the augmented reality/virtual reality market in the not too distant future, as they also offer wearable health monitors, and two or three of them evidently sell phones.

They are all, in short, digital conglomerates, a kind of business that defies industry categorization. In some sense we are back to the future, circa 1980. And to the extent that Big Tech corporations do not fit industry categories, a different way of thinking about their power may be required. We return to this theme in Section 9.

6.4 Big Business vs. Big Tech

Big Tech companies such as Alphabet and Amazon use their expertise in ICTs to make money. They are indifferent to industry boundaries; they look for opportunities to apply ICTs in new ways that yield profits. Because our lives have become thoroughly intermediated by ICTs over the past generation, the opportunities for tech companies are seemingly unlimited, and the dangers created by Big Tech are without precedent. They are not analogous to the railroads, oil, electricity, the telephone, radio, or a superhighway, because ICTs have become inescapable in human interaction: markets, dating, democracy, work, conversation, protests, cooking, parenting, auto repair, medicine. Whatever you are doing, your smartphone is most likely involved.

Big Tech is qualitatively different from other kinds of big business and requires different tools to tame it. Consider how Big Tech and Big Business responded to the January 6, 2021 incursion into the US Capitol by seditionists seeking to overturn the presidential election. Big Business responded by shutting off their cash spigot. Shortly after January 6, corporations such as Marriott, American Express, Dow, Goldman Sachs, AT&T, Best Buy, and Mastercard announced that they were halting political contributions to senators and representatives who voted against certifying the 2020 presidential election – at least for the moment. (The next election was almost two years off.) In contrast, Facebook and Twitter immediately suspended Trump's social media accounts, depriving him of his megaphone. Apple and Google quickly removed Parler, the social media platform used by some of the seditionists, from their app stores.

And Amazon cut off Parler's access to Amazon Web Services, where it had been hosted, thus deleting it from the world. Big Business cut off political funding – at best a symbolic gesture. Big Tech pulled the rug from under Trump and his followers, halting them in their tracks and easing the transition to a new administration (Davis, 2021a).

Even the "bigness" of Big Tech is different. While relatively few people are employed by Google or Facebook – and fewer still by Netflix or Twitter – they have an outsized influence on our culture and economy. As of July 2021, the market capitalization of Alphabet, Amazon, Apple, Facebook, and Microsoft (that is, the total value of their shares on the stock market) made up over one-quarter of the value of the S&P 500 (Neate and Rushe, 2021). Just five corporations carried an astonishing weight, indirectly shaping critical choices around college, retirement, and major purchases. We next turn to the meaning of corporate size.

7 What Is Size Now?

What is America's biggest corporation? The answer depends on what you mean by *big*. The biggest employer in America is Walmart, with 2.3 million workers. The biggest in market capitalization is Apple, valued at just over $2 trillion (but only number 44 in terms of employment). The nonfinancial corporation with the most assets is AT&T, at $526 billion (number 27 in employment and number 28 in market capitalization). And the biggest in sales is, again, Walmart.

We often refer to "giant corporations" in a fairly casual way. We all know what we're talking about, right? But size is an increasingly misleading metaphor to describe corporations. For most of the twentieth century, big corporations were big in all ways. Today, the different meanings of size have become detached, so a company can be a giant in revenues or market capitalization but tiny in assets and employment. It may be time to abandon size as our metaphor for business.

7.1 Who's the Biggest?

Tables 4, 5, and 6 list the ten biggest US corporations in employment, market capitalization, and sales as of May 2021, along with the total annual compensation of their median employee.[57]

You will notice some clear patterns. America's biggest employers are in retail, where wages are very low. Its most valuable companies are in

---

[57] The data in these tables are from Orbis, www.bvdinfo.com/en-us/our-products/data/international/orbis (downloaded May 2021).

Table 4 America's ten largest corporations by employment, 2021[58]

Company	Revenues (millions)	Employees	Market cap (millions)	Compensation
Walmart	559,151	2,300,000	397,486	20,942
Amazon	386,064	1,298,000	1,634,168	29,007
UPS	84,628	543,000	120,442	44,254
Home Depot	132,110	504,800	291,565	27,389
Kroger	132,498	465,000	26,266	24,617
Target	93,561	409,000	90,725	24,535
IBM	73,620	375,300	112,166	49,001
Berkshire Hathaway	245,510	360,000	317,883	68,543
Starbucks	23,518	349,000	100,440	12,113
Lowe's	89,597	340,000	122,255	24,554

Table 5 America's ten largest corporations by market capitalization, 2021

Company	Revenues (millions)	Employees	Market cap (millions)	Compensation
Apple	274,515	147,000	2,007,837	57,783
Amazon	386,064	1,298,000	1,634,168	29,007
Microsoft	143,015	163,000	1,543,306	172,142
Tesla	31,536	70,757	668,905	58,455
Facebook	85,965	58,604	656,668	262,633
Alphabet	182,527	135,301	526,920	273,493
Johnson & Johnson	82,584	134,500	414,310	81,000
Walmart	559,151	2,300,000	397,486	20,942
JPMorgan Chase	119,995	249,184	387,335	80,102
Mastercard	14,980	21,000	352,825	132,114

technology – and technology companies often employ few people, albeit at high wages. (Alphabet's median employee took home twice as much cash as the

---

[58] This list excludes Yum China Holdings whose 400,000 employees work almost exclusively in China.

Table 6 America's ten largest corporations by revenues, 2021

Company	Revenues (millions)	Employees	Market cap (millions)	Compensation
Walmart	559,151	2,300,000	397,486	20,942
Amazon	386,064	1,298,000	1,634,168	29,007
Apple	274,515	147,000	2,007,837	57,783
CVS Health	268,706	300,000	89,399	55,716
United Health Group	257,141	330,000	332,732	55,696
Berkshire Hathaway	245,510	360,000	317,883	68,543
McKesson	238,228	76,000	31,044	40,601
Amerisource Bergen	189,893	22,000	19,785	59,388
Alphabet	182,527	135,301	526,920	273,493
Exxon Mobil	178,574	72,000	174,288	183,234

median employee at Goldman Sachs.) And some of the corporations with the biggest revenues are anonymous middlemen like AmerisourceBergen.

Not every company fits this description. Amazon and Walmart are mammoth on all dimensions – employment, revenues, and market capitalization – but they are distinctive in this respect. The other tech "giants" are mostly giant in market capitalization alone.

Contrast this with the biggest corporations in 1980 (Table 7). For the first four decades after World War II, the biggest businesses were biggest in all respects: sales, employment, assets, and market capitalization. When Fortune magazine began its Fortune 500 list in 1955, General Motors was at the top on all dimensions and represented the prototype of the large American corporation, held to account by an assertive union. The biggest companies provided high wages, generous benefits, and career employment with well-defined job ladders. There was a systematic "large firm wage premium" in which big employers paid better for the same jobs compared to small firms.[59] The best-paying jobs, and the longest career ladders, were in the biggest corporations.

---

[59] See Cobb and Lin (2017) and Bloom et al. (2018) on the disappearing large firm wage premium.

Table 7 America's ten largest corporations by employment, 1980

Company	Revenues (millions)	Employees	Market cap (millions)
AT&T	50,791	847,000	36,137
GM	57,729	746,000	13,950
Ford	37,086	426,000	2,411
GE	24,959	402,000	13,950
Sears	25,195	391,000	4,800
IBM	26,213	341,000	39,625
ITT	18,530	320,000	3,670
Kmart	14,343	256,000	2,200
Mobil	59,510	212,000	17,167
GTE	9,979	201,000	4,200

Today the biggest employers are among the lowest paying, and the job ladders in retail are more like step stools. The highest-paying corporations tend to be light in the number of jobs they offer, and they often rely heavily on contractors rather than full-time employees. As noted in Section 2.4, Alphabet relies primarily on temps, vendors, and contractors rather than full-time employees. Tech firms are especially rigorous about maintaining minimalist employment rolls. The "prepackaged software" companies that have recently gone public typically employ very few people: Airbnb (5,465), Coursera (779), Olo (433), Asana (701), Palantir (2,398), Bentley (4,010), C2.ai (482), and Snowflake (2,037) collectively employed fewer people than Under Armour, America's 400th-biggest corporation (see note 51).

This aversion to creating jobs is a distinctly American phenomenon that dates to choices made in the wake of World War II. America's peculiar system of welfare provision, in which health insurance is provided by employers rather than the government, helps explain the hesitancy around employment. The average annual cost to an employer of providing health insurance to a head of household is over $22,000 (Kaiser Family Foundation, 2021). That is a benefit that would nearly double the employment cost of the average worker at Walmart or Target or Home Depot, and certainly gives pause to any company considering hiring full-time workers. To put it plainly, America's lack of a national healthcare system is a job killer.

7.2 Big, or Loud?

Corporate size is often equated with power: Big corporations can throw their weight around, and some are deemed too big to fail. But which aspect of bigness is it that provides power? Home Depot, Kroger, and Target are three of America's biggest employers, but they are rarely singled out for their political swagger. Drug distributors McKesson and AmerisourceBergen have vast revenues, but this has not shielded them from prosecution for their alleged roles in the opioid epidemic. And even the concept of being "too big to fail," emerging from the 2008 financial crisis, seems a bit too glib, given how many financial giants were, in fact, allowed to fail (or be acquired under duress): Lehman Brothers, Bear Sterns, Merrill Lynch, Wachovia, Washington Mutual, Countrywide, New Century, and many other financial giants evaporated within a brief period around 2008.

Compare these hapless giants with a company that became an inescapable daily companion for hundreds of millions of workers and students during the Covid-19 pandemic: Zoom Video Communications. During 2020 and 2021, like many people, I averaged at least ten hours per week on Zoom in meetings, classes, webinars, virtual cocktail hours, and impromptu catch-ups. (I doubt if I spent ten hours, in total, speaking on the phone during the lockdown.) At the beginning of 2020, relatively few people had even heard of Zoom. One year later, it was the oxygen of the work-from-home economy, scaling from anonymity to ubiquity in a few months, and adding useful features on a weekly basis. Yet its annual report from March 2021 notes that it has just 4,422 employees globally and rents server space from Amazon and Oracle.[60] Put another way, by one crucial measure, Home Depot is more than *100 times bigger* than Zoom.

Minimal assets, few employees, and a market capitalization of over $100 billion – in some sense, Zoom is a prototype of the twenty-first century "big" tech company. Zoom's tiny tangible footprint suggests that size is not a helpful metaphor anymore. Potent tech firms are not big – they are loud (Davis, 2021b). Yet Zoom is also a mystery: Why has it not yet been crushed by evil monopolists? Why are we not all using Apple's FaceTime, Google Hangouts, Facebook Messenger, Microsoft Teams, Amazon … whatever? Why has a (far superior, continuously upgraded) product from out of nowhere

---

[60] United States Securities and Exchange Commission, www.sec.gov/ix?doc=/Archives/edgar/data/0001585521/000158552121000048/zm-20210131.htm

managed to beat the biggest stars of the tech firmament? And if Zoom can do it, can anyone else?

8 Every Man an LLC? The Hollow Promise of Entrepreneurship for All

It is often said that anyone with a credit card and an internet connection can now assemble a business from parts available online – capital, labor, supplies, and distribution. In Section 2, I discussed the example of the Instant Pot, a computerized pressure cooker launched by a tiny team in Ontario that reached a large global market via Amazon. But there are countless examples of such online-first enterprises that assemble digital supply chains through an entirely remote process.

I could have mentioned eyglassdepot.com, an unsavory vendor of designer sunglasses. The one-man company doesn't hold any inventory, but simply collects orders online and passes them off to other (often counterfeit) sellers for fulfillment – and handles customer complaints himself in a distinctive New York style (Segal, 2021). Or I could have gone to Amazon to see dozens of cryptic brands for clothing, toys, electronic products, and more (Herrman, 2020).

The barriers to entry for starting an enterprise online have never been lower. It also seems that many of the most successful ideas were hatched by kids in a dorm room after a few too many bong hits. "What if you could push a button on your phone and some guy would just show up in his car and take you where you want to go, and it would charge your credit card?" (That would be Uber.) "What if you could order a burrito on your phone and it would appear at your door?" (That would be DoorDash.) "What if you could get a vape pen, rolling papers, Ben & Jerry's, and some beer to show up when you ran out?" (That would be GoPuff, currently valued at $9 billion.)

It's not just stoner business models that have become easy to execute. If you have a beer recipe, you can find a vendor to brew it, bottle it, and paste on your label. Your grandma's tomato sauce recipe could be produced by LiDestri of Rochester, New York – like Newman's Own and dozens of store brands. It is trivially easy to start a record label, YouTube channel, clothing line, or flat-screen television brand. With the rise of commissary "ghost kitchens" (e.g., Uber founder Travis Kalanick's new venture, CloudKitchens), anyone with a book of recipes can start a virtual delivery restaurant online. Robinhood demonstrates that you don't need much background in finance to start a fintech business. Fisker shows that you don't need to build a factory to start a car company. (And with the advent of electric car chassis makers, we may see a flood of new auto brands in the coming years, presumably sold on Amazon – see Wilson, 2020.)

Monopoly is not always a barrier to entry. Until recently, the Federal Reserve seemed to have a monopoly on issuing currency in the United States – but these days a new meme-based cryptocurrency seems to pop up weekly.

If anyone can launch a business with modest startup costs, then why are there so few new businesses? The Kauffman Foundation tracks "startup density," the proportion of businesses with at least one employee that are less than a year old. They find that today's startup rates are half what they were in the late 1970s, when Jimmy Carter was US president: "[W]hen compared to the levels in the 1980s, 1990s, and early 2000s, Startup Density is in a long-term decline" (Kauffman Foundation, 2017: 22). Or perhaps we are just measuring it wrong. Judging by applications for Employer Identification Numbers, Census Bureau data suggest that 2020 was a boom year for startups, which increased by 24 percent over the previous year (Zhang, 2021) – even as the failure rate of existing businesses also skyrocketed. Perhaps we are surrounded by startups that we have failed to notice. If I offer haircuts in my garage, or sell self-defense equipment out of my trunk, or write iOS apps on the weekend, or drive for Uber in the evenings, does that count as starting a company? If I change how I report book royalties on my income taxes, does that count as a new business? (According to the Internal Revenue Service (IRS): yes.) If I work as a contractor in construction and create a limited liability company (LLC) to receive my compensation (as some general contractors require), am I now a firm?

As we have learned, many of the categories we use to understand the economy – nationality, industry, size – often fail us in a digital world.

Much of what we know about American business comes from Census Bureau data collected on "establishments." According to the Bureau's definition, "A firm is a business organization consisting of one or more establishments under common ownership or control. *An establishment is a single physical location where business is conducted or where services or industrial operations are performed*" (US Census Bureau, 2017; emphasis added). See the problem? If Coinbase chooses to operate with no physical facilities but just remote employees or contractors, is it not a firm?[61]

If you wanted to assemble information on how many professional basketball games were played in the United States in March 2021 and what the outcomes were, you can do so with a quick internet search. If you're obsessive, you can get data on every player in every game and second-by-second changes in the score. Now imagine collecting similar data on all pickup basketball games played in the United States during the same period. We know they are happening, but we have no way of measuring it systematically. So it is with our ICT-mediated economy. This is especially true when it comes to "entrepreneurship," a slippery concept with no clear definition but with great potential value in pacifying the population as our economy becomes ever more atomized.

8.1 Entrepreneurship as an American Ideology

No country in history has idolized business leaders the way America does. From Thomas Edison and Henry Ford to Jack Welch and Steve Jobs, the administrators who run US commercial enterprises are weirdly venerated. Fans follow Elon Musk's every utterance about the latest crypto fad, titter at his pricing strategies ($69,420 for the Model S? Hilarious!), and zealously defend his honor as the founder of Tesla. (To be clear: Elon Musk is not the founder of Tesla – he joined later as an investor.)

There is perhaps nothing more American than wanting to be your own boss. Thomas Jefferson envisioned a nation of self-sufficient yeoman farmers controlling their own destiny on land that had only recently belonged to America's indigenous peoples. This vision of the small farmer morphed into the small businessman and Main Street shopkeeper. The recent spate of books on the horrors of monopoly describe a lost golden era of local enterprise when the Sherman Act and baroque banking laws protected small towns from urban cosmopolitans back East. Look, there's young Louis Brandeis strolling the idyllic streets of his native Louisville, Kentucky, chatting up the local petit bourgeoisie and enjoying a time evidently free of anti-Semitism.

This enchanted world was threatened by the corporatization of the economy early in the twentieth century. Working for someone else in a giant factory or a chain store would rob men of their vitality. Luckily, there was antitrust to

---

[61] What is a "firm," anyway? According to the CORE Project's book on "The Economy" (www .core-econ.org/the-economy/book/text/06.html), a firm is an "Economic organization in which private owners of capital goods hire and direct labour to produce goods and services for sale on markets to make a profit." Does it matter if the capital goods are rented, or labor is provided by self-employed contractors responding to suggestions from an app? Does requiring kitchen staff to follow a recipe count as "directing labor"?

protect from the accursed efficiencies of large-scale enterprise, allowing the United States to remain a nation of shopkeepers.

In America, entrepreneurship is not just a neutral description of certain forms of commercial activity. It is a noble ideal of self-sufficiency and civic engagement, worthy of protection and nurturance.[62] In that sense, it is a useful tool for easing painful economic transitions. If you can convince an Uber driver that he or she is not an underpaid member of the lumpen proletariat but a self-employed entrepreneur, the rightful heir to Jefferson's yeoman farmer, then you will certainly ease their coming walk through the fire swamp of large-scale labor dislocation.[63] (Uber's ad campaigns to recruit drivers bear this out.)

The problem with the ideology of entrepreneurship is that, like so much else, its stylized facts are simply wrong. Moreover, as we move toward an increasingly atomized online economy of all markets all the time, the ideology of entrepreneurship is likely to serve as a kind of palliative care for a more solidaristic economy.

8.2 Startups and Job Creation

Entrepreneurs are often hailed as job creators. According to the folklore, small businesses – or possibly young businesses – are the source of economic dynamism and job creation. When new enterprises create new products that succeed in the marketplace they raise capital, invest in new plant and equipment, and – crucially – hire people to meet their new demand.[64]

As you might expect by now, this narrative does not hold up well in the twenty-first century, when businesses can quickly scale up by renting supply, distribution, and labor. My analysis of every US business that did an IPO from 2001 to 2015 showed that very few firms subsequently created jobs at any scale. The median company "created" just fifty-one jobs after going public, and often the new jobs were just a reallocation of old jobs via acquisition. The company with the best record at creating genuinely new jobs was GameStop, the strip mall video game retailer whose average nonmanagerial employee earned just $8 per hour (Davis, 2016c).

Even the most successful corporations limit their job growth to the extent possible. I noted in Section 2.4 Alphabet's primary reliance on a contingent workforce that is offered no path to permanent employment (Wakabayashi,

---

[62] See Eberhart, Barley, and Nelson (2021) for an acute dissection of the ideology of entrepreneurship.

[63] See Dubal (2017) for a thoughtful analysis of our evolving employment categories and the functions they serve. Schor (2020) provides a detailed discussion of the gig economy.

[64] See Decker et al. (2014) for an overview of startups, job creation, and the apparent decline in entrepreneurship in the twenty-first-century American economy.

2019). This pattern is repeated across the high-wage tech sector, where permanent full-time employment is relatively scarce.

Moreover, technology is creating an increasingly job-lite workplace. A new gastropub in my hometown of Detroit presents patrons with a QR code on their table. When scanned with a smartphone, customers can view the menu, place their order, and pay via credit card, their conversation only briefly interrupted by an anonymous foodrunner dropping off their food and drink. Two kitchen staff and one foodrunner are sufficient for the entire establishment. Eighteen months into the COVID-19 pandemic, most sit-down restaurants in the United States have added a QR code option to view the menu, or shifted entirely to the server-free model, which is estimated to cut 30–50 percent off labor costs (Woo, 2021). And the remaining staff may not even be employees: Apps like Pared allow restaurants to recruit labor by the shift (Sedacca and Yaffe-Belany, 2019). Given the interoperability of most kitchen roles, it is not crazy to think that the kitchen staff might work at a different venue every night, with prevailing wages shifting according to market conditions.

8.3 Competition and Innovation

A frequent refrain of the anti-monopolists is that competition encourages innovation. Enabling competition via entrepreneurship makes for a healthier economy, they say. Two shoe stores on Main Street make each other better, providing lower prices, friendlier service, better selection, more lush carpeting – far better than what a single shoe store (or perhaps Zappo's) might offer.

Shareholder value capitalism indeed produces a lot of innovation: Juicero, Juul, Oxycontin, WeWork, Mugshots.com, for-profit toddler prisons, valet parking apps, ranch-flavored fentanyl, Farmville, Baby Shark, Ashley Madison, Parler. Americans seemingly benefit from a rich harvest of entrepreneurship. But sometimes we don't need any more innovation. And sometimes competition is not the best path to get the innovation that we do need.

Clearly, competition works in some contexts. In the market for sugar, lead, cars, or military procurement, buyers benefit from robust competition to keep prices down and to incentivize new ways of doing things. But not all markets benefit from adding new competitors. We do not need more opioids, more hyperprocessed foods, more vape pods, more handguns, more petroleum pulled from the earth, more addictive social media, or more for-profit prisons. More is not always better, and broad policies encouraging more entrepreneurship can easily yield more businesses that make us worse off.

Moreover, for some products, monopoly plus collaboration makes the product better. The operating system Linux is arguably a monopoly, but it is given away for free and gets better with each release, improved through volunteer labor. Wikipedia also monopolizes the encyclopedia industry, and it is perhaps the greatest single compilation of human knowledge in history – also free. The coding language Python is not exactly a monopolist, but it gets more useful over time through user-written routines that are shared freely online. And the Instant Pot, although not free itself, benefits from a vast community of enthusiasts who have posted tens of thousands of recipes online, along with countless YouTube videos to walk newbies through them. There are Instant Pot competitors but … why bother? It is durable and cheap, and the recipes are customized to its specific configuration of controls. (These are perhaps also the reasons why Amazon has not created an Instant Pot knockoff yet.)

In short, competition has its place, but it is hardly the only way to promote desirable innovation.

8.4 Sharecropping 2.0

The publisher of *Wired* penned a story in 2018 that contained a soon-to-be immortal line describing the relation between Facebook and traditional media: "Every publisher knows that, at best, they are sharecroppers on Facebook's massive industrial farm" (Thompson, 2018). He was not wrong – quite the contrary. Many media consumers only come to know of an article or video or song because it has been shared on social media – and Facebook controls the platforms and the visibility.

In some sense, sharecropping is an apt description of many business ecosystems today, from meat production to ridehailing. A platform of one sort or another serves as a gatekeeper standing between customers on one side and "entrepreneurs" on the other. But the power that this conveys to the gatekeeper differs by context. Understanding this helps interpret some of the peculiar dynamics that are proliferating as our economy is reorganized.

Uber and Lyft are very clear that the millions of drivers whose cars bear their logo are not employees but independent contractors. Like the chicken farmers who grow broilers on behalf of Tyson, Uber drivers are self-employed entrepreneurs who control their own hours and work conditions and access to health insurance (but not the price at which their service is sold). Their relation to the platform that connects them to customers is as a sovereign, not an employee, and there is no chance that they will wind up being incorporated into the platform.

Amazon and its Marketplace "partners" present a similar situation. Amazon is very good at getting products into the homes of consumers. It is a one-stop shop for distribution for its millions of vendors, each of whom is an independent entrepreneur. Like Uber drivers and TVCs at Alphabet, Marketplace vendors face almost no danger of being acquired by the mother ship (but in some cases a real danger of their product being "emulated").

The situation is different for Big Tech conglomerates and tech startups. Big Tech companies are acquisitive – since 2000 they have made hundreds of acquisitions. Tim Cook was quoted as saying Apple bought a new company every two to three weeks.[65] This is sometimes taken as evidence of monopoly power and industry consolidation in action. But that would be to misunderstand the nature of tech entrepreneurship. Most tech startups are created with the intention of being acquired by Big Tech corporations – this is their preferred "exit strategy" from the start (Arora et al., 2021). (They can also exit by going public, but getting acquired is a surer bet.) Killer acquisitions exist, of course, but far more common is a happy ending for founders and stockholding employees who have achieved their dream, cashed out, and can move on to the next venture. What is being acquired here is intellectual property and, sometimes, talent.

A similar model holds for Big Pharma and biotech. Big Pharma companies like Pfizer and Merck are very good at running drug tests, managing the Food and Drug Administration approval process, and marketing medicines to physicians. In recent times they have been somewhat less good at new drug discovery, for some complicated reasons. Meanwhile, in any given year, a large proportion of IPOs consist of biotech companies that are developing new drugs and other therapies. Many or most will fail; some will come up with breakthroughs. Much like their Little Tech brethren, their dream is not to grow into Big Pharma conglomerates, but to be bought out at a large premium. Being acquired is not a bug; it is a feature for those who develop valuable intellectual property. Acquisition by a massive tech or pharma corporation often provides the surest path to funding and scale and distribution that would otherwise be inaccessible, without the cost of building pointlessly redundant capacity.

For both Big Tech and Big Pharma, the existence of acquisitive platforms like Google and Pfizer does not dampen entrepreneurship. It promotes it by creating a lucrative exit for entrepreneurs, who act as a kind of external R&D department.

ICTs are enabling the "platformization" of more and more markets – creating opportunities for gatekeepers that stand between customers and entrepreneurs. If customers access markets through the Internet, then those who control what is seen on the Internet can shape the market. Call it Sharecropping 2.0.

---

[65] Subcommittee on Antitrust, Commercial and Administrative Law of the Committee on the Judiciary (2020: 337).

Restaurants are one of the most basic forms of entrepreneurship. (There were fast food kiosks in Pompeii.) Nearly every town has at least one restaurant. Immigrant entrepreneurs often start out by opening a restaurant. But DoorDash and its ilk are increasingly inserting themselves between restaurants and customers. Online orders often end up routed through the site of a delivery platform, unbidden by the restaurant itself. DoorDash takes a hefty cut, a slice of which goes to its (nonemployee) drivers. Sometimes this "service" is hard to escape. I recently ordered food to pick up from a restaurant two blocks from my house. Despite my efforts, the order was routed through DoorDash, which made an unwanted substitution that I discovered when I got home.[66] When I returned to the restaurant on foot five minutes later, I was told "We can't help you. Call DoorDash – they handle the orders."

On the Internet nobody knows you are a ghost kitchen, and the COVID-19 pandemic has hastened the creation of virtual delivery restaurants. Chuck E. Cheese outlets across the United States began marketing Pasqually's Pizza & Wings for delivery as a more palatable facade for unwary consumers, and other restaurants began employing their kitchens to create takeout food for their nominal competitors. The natural evolution of this trend is toward commissary kitchens, cuisine-agnostic facilities built for virtual delivery restaurants. Disused buildings or parking lots with ready access for delivery vehicles are ideal. Unlike real-world restaurants, there is no need for walkability or ambience. A given commissary kitchen could in principle cook for dozens of online-only restaurants, just as Foxconn manufactures products for Apple, Amazon, Xiaomi, and Sony. Think of it as Nikefication for food, where menu design is fully separated from production (e.g., CloudKitchens) and distribution (e.g., DoorDash).

In the not too distant future we are likely to see the manufacturing equivalent of the commissary kitchen: the universal fabrication facility. Some industries have already fully detached design and branding from manufacturing – garments, electronics, consumer packaged goods. Foxconn and other companies in the electronics manufacturing services (EMS) sector provided proof of concept that a broad mix of products can be designed anywhere and produced in bulk in the same factory – phones, laptops, routers, webcams. (Coyle and Nguyen [2020] use the evocative term "factoryless manufacturing.") TechShop and other commercial makerspaces have demonstrated that low-cost capital equipment can enable localized production of globally sourced designs. The COVID-19 pandemic has highlighted the dangers of relying on overseas vendors for

---

[66] Note to DoorDash and friends: People who willingly order tofu almost certainly will not accept chicken as a substitute.

crucial products, and ongoing trade tensions militate in favor of reshoring. It is not hard to imagine on-demand manufacturing for certain goods being done by facilities adjacent to Amazon's massive warehouses – not this year, but one day.

We are already much of the way there. The "platformized" sharecropping model is pervasive, and may not be universally disastrous for entrepreneurs – but the language of entrepreneurship is likely to serve as a Trojan horse to sugarcoat some brutal economic transitions (Eberhart et al., 2021). Finally, we consider what makes gatekeepers powerful or dispensable, and how to tame them.

9 What Next? Business Models and Power

The digital revolution is fundamentally reshaping economies around the world by changing the raw materials of business: the input markets for capital, labor, supplies, and distribution, as well as methods of management. ICTs make it feasible to rent rather than own the core components of enterprise, through markets that would have been impossibly costly without the Internet and smartphones. As a result, corporations are far fewer in number and look very different than they did a generation ago. New noncorporate forms are proliferating but are largely invisible due to the way we gather data on the economy. The COVID-19 pandemic has further accelerated the move toward a more dispersed economy.

Public policy defines the rules for how input markets operate, erecting guardrails for how business evolves – for example, by establishing standards for what counts as an employee versus a contractor. This is why the ridehailing industry looks radically different around the world. American shareholder capitalism gives us Uber, a secretive scofflaw with opaque pricing, aggressive political engagement, and an army of precarious nonemployee drivers. But the same technology is implemented very differently in Germany, Sweden, Indonesia, and India.[67] Getting the rules right at the start is essential.

Over the course of the twentieth century, America reined in its corporations by regulating the markets in which they participate: antitrust law (shaping how companies compete with each other and engage their suppliers), finance law (for banking and securities), labor law (for employment and unions), and corporate law (how corporations are created and governed). During the Nixon years, regulation reached directly into their operations: the Occupational Safety and Health Administrationto protect workers from harm, the Equal Employment Opportunity Commission to make employment equitable, the Consumer

---

[67] Thelen (2018) and Davis and Sinha (2021) analyze how the Uber model was implemented in different countries around the world.

Product Safety Commission to keep a company's products safe, the Environmental Protection Agency to reduce the negative environmental impact of business, and others. Regulations were squarely aimed at large, vertically integrated, exchange-listed, US-based corporations as the modal form of enterprise. But as we have seen, this twentieth-century format no longer fits the twenty-first-century economy.

Recent discussions of American capitalism are tinged with nostalgia for old-timey antitrust. Some antitrust champions yearn to return to a golden age of Main Street commerce that evidently lasted for a few weeks in 1950. They insist that more competitive markets will set us free. But, as Konczal (2021) argues, sometimes freedom requires us to be protected from markets. In American capitalism, cheap wins – competitive markets get us to the cheapest price, and ICTs enable markets for everything. We may not, however, love the results.

Think of how your work life would change if every day you competed for a shift at your job in an online auction where the lowest bidder wins. Such a situation may not be far off, whether you are a teacher, a dishwasher, or an emergency room physician. Uber has the technology – It takes only the will, and some legal tweaking, to unleash an Ayn Rand worker's utopia. Most everyone will be a self-employed entrepreneur running their own small (tiny, micro) business, and our yeoman dishwasher will create an LLC to receive their wage, which will vary from day-to-day according to market conditions. That may be a less corporate, more market-friendly future, but it will not be a better one.

9.1 New Century, New Forms of Corporate Power

In the twentieth century, corporate power came from size and concentration. Dominant corporations were those that were the biggest in the steel or auto or telecom or investment banking industry. But we have left that century behind. Kenney and Zysman (2016: 62) put it well: "We are in the midst of a reorganization of our economy in which the platform owners are seemingly developing power that may be even more formidable than was that of the factory owners in the early industrial revolution."

In a world where economic activities are increasingly mediated online, power flows not from size (however defined) but from being a gatekeeper. We find ourselves in an unfamiliar situation where powerful new entities arise as if out of nowhere, from a garage or a dorm room. The recent report of the University of Chicago's Stigler Committee on Digital Platforms (2019: 7–8) describes these peculiar new domains:

> The markets where DPs operate exhibit several economic features that, while not novel per se, appear together for the first time and push these markets

towards monopolization by a single company. These features are: i) strong network effects (the more people use a product, the more appealing this product becomes for other users); ii) strong economies of scale and scope (the cost of producing more or of expanding in other sectors decreases with company's size); iii) marginal costs close to zero (the cost of servicing another consumer is close to zero); (iv) high and increasing returns to the use of data (the more data you control, the better your product); and v) low distribution costs that allow for a global reach. This confluence of features means that these markets are prone to tipping; that is, they reach a point where the market will naturally tend towards a single, very dominant player (also known as "winner takes all markets").

The source of power in these settings is not being the tallest building but being at the right intersection. Most tech firms are not significant gatekeepers, whatever their "bigness." There are simply not that many profitable business models that lend themselves to being a bottleneck. If riders and drivers both have Uber and Lyft on their phones ("multihoming"), then neither is a gatekeeper. If a dozen firms can offer commission-free online trading of stocks, or free videoconferencing, or music streaming, or electric scooter rental, then none is a gatekeeper.

Corporations do not need to be gatekeepers to misbehave. Nonmonopolists can be oppressive employers and noxious polluters and terrible citizens, peddling useless and dangerous products that make the world a worse place. There are plenty of evil business models that do not involve monopoly but still impose great costs on society.

But there are some kinds of gatekeepers that are particularly crucial to the economy and require greater scrutiny. Perhaps the most potent are those that control access to the building blocks of business: capital, labor, supplies, and distribution.[68] Addressing the challenges created by gatekeepers in these domains is essential for getting the guardrails right.

We also want to keep in mind the long game. Facebook's latest outrage or Amazon's horrifying new patent are most salient today, but we are laying the foundations for the organization of the economy to come. Edmonton-based athlete Wayne Gretzky famously said, "A good hockey player plays where the puck is. A great hockey player plays where the puck is going to be." We have the technology to create a more democratic and equitable economy, and we also have a widespread consensus that corporate power is out of control. Let's use this opportunity to create the world we want, not just to give Pop Sockets a better placement on Amazon, or to get more dating apps on Google Play.

---

[68] Rahman (2017) suggests that companies that are large in scale, provide significant inputs to other industries, and are able to limit access to vulnerable customers deserve particular legal scrutiny.

9.2 The Monopoly Narrative Is Misguided

Partisans on the left and right have converged on a monopoly narrative in recent years. In its stylized form, it goes like this: After Professor Bork (1978) published his treatise, antitrust in America fell into a coma, which unshackled an economic centripetal force that left nearly every industry dominated by monopolists. Monopolists drive up prices, drive down wages, make worse products, throttle innovation, and exercise unconstrained political power. The best policy response is to locate big companies, cut them down to size, and encourage more markets and more competition wherever possible.

As I have argued in this Element, the monopoly narrative gets many things wrong. For two decades after Bork's book, American industry became less concentrated, and corporations outsourced wherever they could. Since then, the digital transformation has scrambled the very idea of "industry" and "size" and "market share" – not to mention "nationality," "firm," and "employee." The corporation itself is an increasingly obsolete way to organize economic activity in the United States, and there are half as many as there were twenty-five years ago.

What happened? The digital revolution enabled more robust markets in successive domains. Capital markets (financialization), supply markets (Nikefication), distribution channels (Amazon), and labor markets (Uberization) have been fundamentally transformed in waves since the early 1980s. At the same time, the corporation itself has been transformed, shifting from a social institution to a financial vehicle singularly driven to create shareholder value. American shareholder capitalism is a machine exquisitely fine-tuned to create profit, whatever its source and whatever the outcome for society. Corporations that fail to heed the command to create shareholder value face swift retribution from outside investors. Monopoly can be a useful tool for generating shareholder value, but it is hardly the only one. To revisit our earlier compendium, opioids, hyperprocessed food, nicotine pods, and petroleum can all be both competitive and profitable.

The danger of the consensus monopoly narrative is that it prescribes more markets and more competition as the solution to our ills. Markets have their proper place, but that place is not "everywhere." Markets are intrinsically disruptive. Consider how the meaning of a date is different if money changes hands. Or a kidney donation. Or the adoption of a child. For-profit toddler prisons on the border with Mexico may be less costly than government-run facilities, but cost is not the only thing we value.

ICTs are enabling markets in ever more domains of social life. But, to paraphrase Ronald Reagan, in this present crisis, markets are not the solution to our problem – markets *are* the problem. And if Josh Hawley shares your diagnosis of the situation, you should probably be anxious.

9.3 Antitrust Will Not Fix What Ails American Capitalism

Lina Khan's (2017) brilliant article "Amazon's Antitrust Paradox" sets the terms of the current debate around monopoly in the tech sector. She says: "If it is true that the economics of platform markets may encourage anticompetitive market structures, there are at least two approaches we can take. Key is deciding whether we want to govern online platform markets through competition, or want to accept that they are inherently monopolistic or oligopolistic and regulate them instead" (Khan 2017: 790). The first favors antitrust and perhaps breakups as a remedy; the second, regulation.

Let's compare those approaches. Antitrust is slow, unreliable, and unlikely to survive scrutiny by courts that have been packed with Borkies for the past four decades. The limitations of antitrust are not just due to the narcotic effect of Robert Bork's long-out-of-print writings. Wheeler et al. (2020: 25) point out that, "It's not realistic to expect antitrust to have an important influence on privacy, data security, hate speech, imminent incitements to violence, malign foreign influence, or misinformation," particularly if we need action soon. Antitrust cases commonly drag on for years and often end up before judges who are unimpressed. This is not just because so many judges (including a preponderance of current Supreme Court justices) have been marinated in Chicago School orthodoxy, although that does not help. It was an Obama-appointed federal judge who threw out the FTC's initial case against Facebook in June 2021, pointing out that just because conventional wisdom calls it a monopolist this does not make it so under the law (Kang, 2021). Crane (2020) argues that the long history of antitrust in America shows Congress passing broad statutes seemingly aimed at reining in corporate power, and courts deciding matters much more narrowly and pragmatically. There is no point in passing high-minded legislation if its practical impact is rendered negligible by the courts.

It is not just the monopoliness of Facebook that makes it bad: It is Facebook's noxious business model based on selling advertisements. If finely targeted outrage and titillation and echo chambers drive engagement, and engagement enables Facebook to sell more ads, then it is not hard to predict what it will do. Whistleblower Frances Haugen shared internal documents demonstrating that insiders are quite familiar with the horrifying collateral damage of Facebook's business model – but boy, is it great for shareholder value (Oremus, 2021). Facebook is a for-profit business. Moreover, antitrust is often far too indirect for the kinds of problems it is being asked to solve. Critics argue that Facebook was much more rigorous about protecting the privacy of user data when it had competitors. But it is hard to believe that the surest path to better user privacy is to demand that Facebook spin off Instagram, thereby creating a vigorous competitive struggle that will ultimately yield greater user privacy several years down the road. Or that more competition will produce a better solution to what should be done about Trump and social media. Using antitrust to address these problems is like trying to do surgery wearing oven mitts.

Google Search is a natural monopoly, and promoting a revival of Lycos, Alta Vista, and AskJeeves would not yield better search results. Instead, it would impose a burden on website owners who have to endure being crawled by endless bots seeking to create a map of the web as comprehensive as Google's. (If you are wondering why so many websites ask you whether you are a robot, now you know. Google and Microsoft crawlers get waved in; the rest of us have to make it past a doorman, including the web-crawlers of prospective competitors to Google Search.) But there is no inherent noncommercial reason for Google Search to create horrifyingly intrusive profiles of its users to sell targeted ads. As with Facebook, Google turned into a surveillance capitalist in order to sell ads. Surveillance capitalism turns out to be just shareholder capitalism plus online surveillance (see Morozov, 2019; Zuboff, 2019).

How about Amazon? From a consumer's perspective, Amazon is a miracle unto the Lord. Think back to how many hours you might have spent shopping for Ford Fusion hubcaps, headphones, cat litter, and vitamin D before Amazon. Do you really want to drive to the mall and wander through Sears rather than spend more time with your family? How many hours do you want to spend trying to find a parking space on Main Street to patronize the friendly local pharmacy and shoe store, only to find that they are out of stock? And how well would Americans have survived the COVID-19 pandemic without delivery services on a massive scale? There is good reason why consumer-welfare oriented antitrust has led to a consumer's paradise (albeit a nightmare for labor and the environment).

9.4 Fight the Real Enemy

The Biden Administration has unleashed the most sweeping effort to rein in corporate power since the time of Wilson and Brandeis over a century ago. Biden's July 2021 "Executive Order on Promoting Competition in the American Economy" established "a whole-of-government effort to promote competition in the American economy. The Order includes 72 initiatives by more than a dozen federal agencies to promptly tackle some of the most pressing competition problems across our economy."[69] These efforts range from encouraging the FTC to enforce antitrust laws more aggressively, particularly in Big Tech, to allowing hearing aids to be sold over the counter and third-party repair shops to fix phones and tractors. The initiatives are a wildly diverse grab bag, as if a giant suggestion box of consumer grievances had been tossed into a single policy lashed together by a theme of competition.

Many of the proposed initiatives will help consumers, workers, or both. As a citizen, I would be delighted to see many of these policies enacted. But to the extent that there is a coherent theory underlying this effort, it is the misguided monopoly narrative and the "curse of bigness," for which the cure is thought to be more competition. Like the many recent anti-monopoly books, Biden's executive order relies on the same narrative and the same problematic evidence to justify its proposals, headed by the claim that 75 percent of industries have become more concentrated, as featured in the second paragraph of the "Fact Sheet."

We are living through a radical reorganization of the economy, driven in large part by ICTs. Because software is eating the world, markets are eating the world. If we want to guide the development of the economy in a humane and democratic direction in the face of this tectonic shift, a shotgun approach simply will not work. "Promoting competition" in an economy driven by shareholder value will not yield stable jobs, healthy communities, or a stronger democracy. Public policy needs to be grounded in a forward-looking sense of what enterprise can and should look like.

For the most pressing problems created by Big Tech, there are several recent proposals that draw on experiences in other industries and countries to limit the power of our tech oligarchs. The simplest solution to noxious ad-based business models is to tax targeted online ads, as Maryland and other states are now endeavoring to do. Economist Paul Romer has proposed exactly this: a progressive tax on targeted digital ads, according to the theory that if you want less of something, tax it (Romer, 2019).[70] Stoller et al. (2020) go further, proposing a ban on targeted advertising to discourage intrusive data collection on users. Business models will adapt to these new realities, perhaps by shifting to subscription income and scrapping the surveillance. Remove the incentive to conduct intrusive data collection, and the problem may solve itself.[71]

---

[69] The White House, Fact Sheet: Executive Order on Promoting Competition in the American Economy (July 9, 2021), www.whitehouse.gov/briefing-room/statements-releases/2021/07/09/fact-sheet-executive-order-on-promoting-competition-in-the-american-economy/.

[70] Romer describes his proposal in more detail in his Capitalisn't Podcast (Romer, 2021).

[71] One option to ease the shift away from ad-based business models is to give Facebook and Google the franchise to collect income taxes on the top 1 percent of earners, for a 0.5 percent fee. This might put their competences to good use while overcoming the budget limitations of the IRS.

Recent proposals to target outrages more specific to Facebook are to regulate the algorithm that determines what shows up in one's newsfeed in what order. This could be done by eliminating protections from liability for feeding particular kinds of content: those that promote discrimination against protected classes, or civil rights violations, or terrorism, or medical misinformation. Alternatively, Facebook could be required to open up the algorithm to enable third-party services to determine the order of the newsfeed, perhaps shaped by user preferences (Oremus, 2021). Doctorow (2021) points out that requiring tech companies to be better at filtering what their users see is unlikely to work as expected; for instance, algorithms generally cannot tell the difference between copyright infringement (which is illegal) and parody (which is not). Moreover, it would inherently advantage incumbent tech giants that can afford to build these costly services. Instead, Doctorow proposes implementing mandatory interoperability – requiring competitive compability that opens up the incumbents' operations to competing services so that, for instance, a user could leave Facebook, take their data with them, and still communicate with their erstwhile platform-friends. Such a landscape would encourage new entrants with innovative services not beholden to our current tech overlords.

A bipartisan group of senators led by Amy Klobuchar and Chuck Grassley has also proposed legislation to prevent Amazon, Apple, Facebook, and Google from self-preferencing their own company's products. Thus, Google could not place Alphabet products inappropriately high in search results, and Amazon could not preference Amazon Basics (Zakrzewski, 2021).

As this brief discussion illustrates, the range of grievances against Big Tech is like a Swiss army knife of offenses: privacy violations, targeted ads, content served up to enrage or to advantage the incumbents' own offerings. The broader problem of the tech economy is the one identified by the Stigler Center report (Stigler Committee on Digital Platforms, 2019): the tendency for certain kinds of ICT-enabled activities to became natural monopolies, or more aptly "gatekeepers." As with data privacy, European regulators took this issue on long before Americans considered it. The European Commission's Digital Markets Act (DMA) creates an explicit designation of a "gatekeeper," identified using quantitative criteria – annual revenues, market capitalization, number of users, and geographic spread of activities. Gatekeepers then become subject to a set of obligations aimed at preserving competition in their markets. Caffara and Scott Morton (2021) note that "Intuitively, we think of a gatekeeper as an intermediary who essentially controls access to critical constituencies on either side of a platform that cannot be reached otherwise, and as a result can engage in conduct and impose rules that counterparties cannot avoid." But they also point out that the implications of being a gatekeeper are not the same across all markets, and that regulators ought to approach them differently depending on their underlying business model: ad-funded platforms (Google Search, Facebook); transaction or market-making platforms (Uber, Amazon); operating systems (iOS, Android, Windows, Amazon Web Services).

I would add that the core markets for enterprises are particularly fraught and require special scrutiny: those for capital, labor, supply, and distribution. At the moment, markets for capital and labor appear least prone to "gatekeeperization," while distribution (via Amazon, in particular) is most troubling.

Given the evident limits of antitrust for Big Tech, the smartest proposal to address the power of gatekeepers is to create a new regulatory agency along the lines of the Federal Communications Commission or the Consumer Financial Protection Bureau: a Digital Platform Agency (DPA) that would be as nimble as the entities it governed. Detailed arguments for such an agency emerged from a University of Chicago task force on the digital economy (Stigler Committee on Digital Platforms, 2019) and were refined in a recent white paper from the Harvard Kennedy School (Wheeler et al., 2020). As the authors put it, "Neither antitrust nor traditional regulatory tools are capable of moving nimbly or quickly enough, let alone reliably enough, to address immediate impediments to competition and fair dealing that result from the power of dominant digital platforms" (Wheeler et al., 2020: 38). Instead, they propose a new style of agency whose approach would draw on two long-standing common law approaches: the duty of care and the duty to deal. The duty of care establishes responsibility for providers of goods and services to find and mitigate bad outcomes from their use. The duty to deal requires those who provide essential services to allow nondiscriminatory access to those services. These old principles have evident applications to digital platforms.

There are many precedents for creating new regulatory agencies for new industries, starting with the railroads and including drugs, communications, and air travel. The Wheeler et al. (2020) design for a DPA draws thoughtfully on the history of these prior organizations. The proposal is also attentive to the peculiarities of the digital economy, including its extremely rapid and ongoing evolution, as well as the depth of the intertwining of information technology and our daily lives today.

The underappreciated threat (or opportunity) unleashed by new technology is not around product markets but around labor markets. The COVID-19 pandemic has revealed just how much work can be done from anywhere, and there is every reason to expect that more and more firms will rely on contract labor recruited from remote locales – including outside the United States. It is not the threat of monopsony in labor markets (that is, a big local employer providing an outsize share of the jobs) that worries me – it is the threat that "jobs" in a particular place will be replaced by "tasks" that are completed by a shifting crew of nonemployee contractors. Nothing would do more to "promote competition in the American economy" than having ongoing bidding wars for shifts by desperate contractors around the world, driving wages to an irreducible minimum that varied from day-to-day. Anyone familiar with the folkways of online labor knows what a nightmare scenario this would be (see Gray and Suri, 2019).

9.5 This Time, How about More Democracy?

A Pigovian tax on targeted ads will help tame some of the horrors of our new surveillance economy. Interoperability will open incumbents up to new competition. A DPA could help address the excesses of our new tech overlords. But we face a bigger threat, and a bigger opportunity.

The COVID-19 pandemic demonstrated just how fully intermediated by Silicon Valley our lives have become, relying on electronic technologies for our most basic human activities. Kindergartners found themselves on lengthy Zoom calls with their teachers and youthful colleagues while their frazzled parents were ordering daily essentials from Instacart and hoping that their work colleagues did not realize they were dialed in from the bathroom. Human contact was limited to desultory cocktail hour FaceTime calls. For many of us, our knowledge of what was going on in the outside world was entirely filtered through apps and social media. Culture was absorbed by streaming dystopian fiction that did not look all that different from COVID life. Tesla's $1.5 billion investment in Bitcoin was responsible for more carbon emissions than all the carbon savings from every car they ever made. Whatever happened to that noisy orange guy who used to be on Twitter all the time? Has Zuckerberg been replaced by an emotionless replicant? Was Qanon renewed for another season?

It does not have to be this way. We have the technologies in hand to create a more sustainable, more inclusive, more equitable, and more democratic economy. We could create human-scale enterprises that meet the needs of our human community; build democracy and accountability into the daily operations of the workplace; fairly compensate care workers for their essential labor; reduce work hours to enable a more balanced life; and start to build a "cosmopolitan locavore" community that is both global and local. But we will not get there as long as shareholder capitalism reigns over us, nor will more markets and more competition get us closer. It is time to privilege democracy over markets.

Under shareholder capitalism, smartphones in labor markets create precarity (for on-demand labor markets such as Uber) or management control (as an electronic leash for intrusive monitoring of workers). But the same technology could just as easily be used to increase democracy and worker control (see Ferreras, 2017). Hayek might have pointed out that there is a lot of knowledge spread throughout an organization. Now we have a low-cost means of aggregating it, to share information and make choices. Online polls are pervasive – why not at work? The recent spread of democratic social movements in tech firms indicate that times have changed. In November 2018, 20,000 Google workers walked off the job to protest the corporation's failure to live up to its values of equity. Salesforce employees demanded that the company cut its ties to the US Customs and Border Protection Agency because they did not want the technology they created to aid in imprisoning toddlers at the border. Microsoft workers sought to cancel a Pentagon contract to develop augmented reality goggles for battlefield use. Around 1,500 Amazon employees walked off the job as part of a climate strike, in part due to the company's dealings with petroleum companies. And in the summer of 2020 Facebook workers demanded that Trump be deplatformed for his use of the service to undermine American democracy (Davis, 2021d). What detractors call "woke capitalism" is spreading through the tech sector and beyond.

Ironically, at the same time democracy is spreading at the grassroots, autocracy is spreading at the apex. Nearly half the tech firms that have gone public in the past few years have given their founders excessive voting rights – often ten or twenty votes per share – that guarantee their personal control and drastically diminish the power of those outside the executive suite, including their own shareholders. Under a peculiar Ayn Rand-inflected theory about the special value of visionary founders, the American venture capital industry is creating a corporate sector that is less and less democratically accountable (Davis, 2021c).

Let's not waste this moment. There is a broad consensus on the hazards of corporate power, and there is righteous anger at the autocrats of Silicon Valley. But the path to a better society is not through more competition and more markets. What we need most now is more democracy.

References

Abril, Danielle, and Drew Harwell. 2021. "Keystroke Tracking, Screenshots, and Facial Recognition: The Boss May Be Watching Long after the Pandemic Ends." *The Washington Post*. September 27. www.washingtonpost.com/tech nology/2021/09/24/remote-work-from-home-surveillance/.

Alchian, Armen A., and Harold Demsetz. 1972. "Production, Information Costs, and Economic Organization." *American Economic Review* 62(5):777–95.

Andreessen, Marc. 2011. "Why Software Is Eating the World." *The Wall Street Journal*. August 20. www.wsj.com/articles/SB100014240531119034 8090457651225091562946.

Arora, Ashish, Andrea Fosfuri, and Thomas Rønde. 2021. "Waiting for the Payday? The Market for Startups and the Timing of Entrepreneurial Exit." *Management Science* 67(3):1453–67. doi: https://doi.org/10.1287/mnsc.2020 .3627.

Athreya, Bama. 2021. "Opinion: A Victory for Gig Workers As California Rules Uber Can't Hack Labor Laws." *Common Dreams*. August 23. www.common dreams.org/views/2021/08/23/victory-gig-workers-california-rules-uber-cant-hack-labor-laws.

Autor, David, David Dorn, Lawrence F. Katz, Christina Patterson, and John Van Reenen. 2020. "The Fall of the Labor Share and the Rise of Superstar Firms." *The Quarterly Journal of Economics* 135(2):645–709. doi: https://doi.org/ 10.1093/qje/qjaa004.

Bacani, Emmanuel Louis. 2020. "S&P 500 Companies' Non-US Revenue Share Hits 10-Year Low – Goldman Sachs." *Accelerating Progress*. June 18. www.spglobal.com/marketintelligence/en/news-insights/latest-news-headlines/s-p-500-companies-non-us-revenue-share-hits-10-year-low-8211-goldman-sachs-59094991.

Barbaro, Michael. 2007. "Wal-Mart Puts Some Muscle behind Power-Sipping Bulbs." *The New York Times*. January 2. www.nytimes.com/2007/01/02/business/02bulb.html.

Berry, Steven, Martin Gaynor, and Fiona Scott Morton. 2019. "Do Increasing Markups Matter? Lessons from Empirical Industrial Organization." *Journal of Economic Perspectives* 33(3):44–68. doi: https://doi.org/10.1257/jep.33.3.44.

Bloom, Nicholas, Fatih Guvenen, Benjamin S. Smith, Jae Song, and Till von Wachter. 2018. "The Disappearing Large-Firm Wage Premium." *AEA Papers and Proceedings* 108:317–22.

Bork, Robert H. 1978. *The Antitrust Paradox: A Policy at War with Itself.* New York: Basic.

Bracken, Becky. 2021. "Darkside Getting Taken to 'Hackers' Court' for Not Paying Affiliates." *Threatpost English Global Threatpostcom.* May 21. https://threatpost.com/darkside-hackers-court-paying-affiliates/166393/.

Broderick, Ryan. 2019. "Forget the Trade War. Tiktok Is China's Most Important Export Right Now." *BuzzFeed News.* May 16. www.buzzfeed news.com/article/ryanhatesthis/forget-the-trade-war-tiktok-is-chinas-most-important-export.

Caffarra, Cristina, and Fiona Scott Morton. 2021. "The European Commission Digital Markets Act: A Translation." *VoxEU.* January 5. https://voxeu.org/article/european-commission-digital-markets-act-translation.

Cameron, Lindsey. 2021. "(Relative) Choice in Algorithms: How Digital Platforms Repurpose Workplace Consent." Unpublished, Wharton School, University of Pennsylvania.

Chandler, Alfred Dupont. 1977. *The Visible Hand: The Managerial Revolution in American Business.* Cambridge, MA: Belknap Press of Harvard University Press.

Coase, Ronald H. 1937. "The Nature of the Firm." *Economica* 4(16):386–405. doi: https://doi.org/10.1111/j.1468-0335.1937.tb00002.x.

Cobb, J. Adam, and Ken-Hou Lin. 2017. "Growing Apart: The Changing Firm-Size Wage Premium and Its Inequality Consequences." *Organization Science* 28(3):429–46. doi: https://doi.org/10.1287/orsc.2017.1125.

Council of Economic Advisors. 2015. "Worker Voice in a Time of Rising Inequality." October. https://obamawhitehouse.archives.gov/sites/default/files/page/files/worker_voice_issue_brief_cea.pdf.

Coyle, Diane, and David Nguyen. 2020. "No Plant, No Problem? Factoryless Manufacturing, Economic Measurement and National Manufacturing Policies." *Review of International Political Economy.* doi: https://doi.org/10.1080/09692290.2020.1778502.

Crane, Daniel. 2020. "Fascism and Monopoly." *Michigan Law Review* 118(7):1315–70. doi: https://doi.org/10.36644/mlr.118.7.fascism.

Crane, Daniel. 2021. "Antitrust Antitextualism." *Notre Dame Law Review* 96(7): 1205.

Davis, Gerald F. 2005. "New Directions in Corporate Governance." *Annual Review of Sociology* 31(1):143–62. doi: https://doi.org/10.1146/annurev.soc.31.041304.122249.

Davis, Gerald F. 2009. *Managed by the Markets: How Finance Reshaped America.* Oxford: Oxford University Press.

Davis, Gerald F. 2010. "Not Just a Mortgage Crisis: How Finance Maimed Society." *Strategic Organization* 8(1):75–82. doi: https://doi.org/10.1177/1476127009355857.

Davis, Gerald F. 2016a. "Can an Economy Survive without Corporations? Technology and Robust Organizational Alternatives." *Academy of Management Perspectives* 30(2):129–40. doi: https://doi.org/10.5465/amp.2015.0067.

Davis, Gerald F. 2016b. *The Vanishing American Corporation: Navigating the Hazards of a New Economy*. First edition. Oakland, CA: Berrett-Koehler Publishers.

Davis, Gerald F. 2016c. "Capital Markets and Job Creation in the 21st Century." Brookings Institution. July 28. www.brookings.edu/research/capital-markets-and-job-creation-in-the-21st-century/.

Davis, Gerald F. 2017. "Post-Corporate: The Disappearing Corporation in the New Economy." *Third Way*. February 1. www.thirdway.org/report/post-corporate-the-disappearing-corporation-in-the-new-economy.

Davis, Gerald F. 2021a. "Big Tech's Swift Reaction to Capitol Rioters Reveals New Face of Corporate Political Power – and a Threat to American Democracy." *The Conversation*. January 19. https://theconversation.com/big-techs-swift-reaction-to-capitol-rioters-reveals-new-face-of-corporate-political-power-and-a-threat-to-american-democracy-153061.

Davis, Gerald F. 2021b. "Big or Loud? We Need New Ways to Define Where the Power Lies." *I by IMD*. March 22. https://iby.imd.org/magazine/big-or-loud-we-need-new-ways-to-define-where-the-power-lies/.

Davis, Gerald F. 2021c. "Ayn Rand-Inspired 'Myth of the Founder' Puts Tremendous Power in Hands of Big Tech CEOS like Zuckerberg – Posing Real Risks to Democracy." *The Conversation*. March 30. https://theconversation.com/ayn-rand-inspired-myth-of-the-founder-puts-tremendous-power-in-hands-of-big-tech-ceos-like-zuckerberg-posing-real-risks-to-democracy-150830.

Davis, Gerald F. 2021d. "Corporate Purpose Needs Democracy." *Journal of Management Studies* 58(3):902–13. doi: https://doi.org/10.1111/joms.12659.

Davis, Gerald F., and Suntae Kim. 2015. "Financialization of the Economy." *Annual Review of Sociology* 41(1):203–21. doi: https://doi.org/10.1146/annurev-soc-073014-112402.

Davis, Gerald F., and Mark S. Mizruchi. 1999. "The Money Center Cannot Hold: Commercial Banks in the U.S. System of Corporate Governance." *Administrative Science Quarterly* 44(2):215. doi: https://doi.org/10.2307/2666995.

Davis, Gerald F., and Aseem Sinha. 2021. "Varieties of Uberization: How Technology and Institutions Change the Organization(s) of Late Capitalism." *Organization Theory* 2(1):263178772199519. doi: https://doi.org/10.1177/2631787721995198.

Davis, Gerald F., and Suzanne K. Stout. 1992. "Organization Theory and the Market for Corporate Control: A Dynamic Analysis of the Characteristics of Large Takeover Targets, 1980–1990." *Administrative Science Quarterly* 37(4):605. doi: https://doi.org/10.2307/2393474.

Davis, Gerald F., Kristina A. Diekmann, and Catherine H. Tinsley. 1994. "The Decline and Fall of the Conglomerate Firm in the 1980s: The Deinstitutionalization of an Organizational Form." *American Sociological Review* 59(4):547. doi: https://doi.org/10.2307/2095931.

De Loecker, Jan, Jan Eeckhout, and Gabriel Unger. 2020. "The Rise of Market Power and the Macroeconomic Implications." *The Quarterly Journal of Economics* 135(2):561–644. doi: https://doi.org/10.1093/qje/qjz041.

Dean, Sam. 2020. "Grindr's New Owners Are Straight. They Say That's OK." *Los Angeles Times*. July 2. www.latimes.com/business/story/2020-07-02/grindr-new-ownership-american-investors-interview.

DeBord, Matthew. 2021. "If You Want to See the Auto Industry's Real Disrupter, Ignore Tesla. Look at Fisker." *Business Insider*. April 23. www.businessinsider.com/the-biggest-disrupter-in-auto-industry-isnt-tesla-its-fisker-2021-3.

Decker, Ryan, John Haltiwanger, Ron Jarmin, and Javier Miranda. 2014. "The Role of Entrepreneurship in US Job Creation and Economic Dynamism." *Journal of Economic Perspectives* 28(3):3–24. doi: https://doi.org/10.1257/jep.28.3.3.

Doctorow, Cory. 2020. *How to Destroy Surveillance Capitalism*. OneZero. https://onezero.medium.com/how-to-destroy-surveillance-capitalism-8135e6744d59.

Doctorow, Cory. 2021. "Competitive Compatibility: Let's Fix the Internet, Not the Tech Giants." *Communications of the ACM* 64(10):26–29. doi: https://doi.org/10.1145/3446789.

Drucker, Jesse. 2009. "Accenture Is Seeking to Change Tax Locales." *The Wall Street Journal*. May 28. www.wsj.com/articles/SB124338175183056465.

Dubal, Veena B. 2017. "Wage Slave or Entrepreneur?: Contesting the Dualism of Legal Worker Identities." *California Law Review* 105(1):65. doi: https://doi.org/10.15779/Z38M84X.

Eberhart, Robert, Stephen Barley, and Andrew Nelson. 2021. "Freedom Is Just Another Word for Nothing Left to Lose: Entrepreneurialism and the Changing Nature of Employment Relations." *Research in the Sociology of Organizations*: *Reversing the Arrow*. August 13. https://ssrn.com/abstract=3904624.

Edelson, Josh. 2021. "The Gig Economy Is Coming for Millions of American Jobs." *Bloomberg.com*. February 17. www.bloomberg.com/news/features/2021-02-17/gig-economy-coming-for-millions-of-u-s-jobs-after-california-s-uber-lyft-vote.

Facebook. 2021. "Terms of Service." www.facebook.com/terms.php (accessed November 27, 2021).

Ferreras, Isabelle. 2017. *Firms as Political Entities: Saving Democracy through Economic Bicameralism*. Cambridge and New York: Cambridge University Press.

Goodnough, Abby. 2021. "Overdose Deaths Have Surged during the Pandemic, C.D.C. Data Shows." *The New York Times*. April 14. www.nytimes.com/2021/04/14/health/overdose-deaths-fentanyl-opiods-coronaviurs-pandemic.html.

Gray, Mary L., and Siddharth Suri. 2019. *Ghost Work: How to Stop Silicon Valley from Building a New Global Underclass*. Boston, MA: Houghton Mifflin Harcourt.

Grullon, Gustavo, Yelena Larkin, and Roni Michaely. 2019. "Are US Industries Becoming More Concentrated?" *Review of Finance* 23(4):697–743. doi: https://doi.org/10.1093/rof/rfz007.

Gurley, Lauren Kaori. 2021. "Amazon's AI Cameras Are Punishing Drivers for Mistakes They Didn't Make." *VICE*. September 20. www.vice.com/en/article/88npjv/amazons-ai-cameras-are-punishing-drivers-for-mistakes-they-didnt-make.

Gutiérrez, Germán, and Thomas Philippon. 2017. "Declining Competition and Investment in the U.S." NBER Working Paper 23583. doi: https://doi.org/10.3386/w23583.

Harnett, Sam. 2021. "'Coming for You and Your Job': With Prop. 22, Are Grocery Staff Layoffs Just the Beginning?" *KQED*. January 20. www.kqed.org/news/11855985/coming-for-you-and-your-job-with-prop-22-are-grocery-staff-layoffs-just-the-beginning.

Hawkins, Andrew J. 2019. "Uber Argues Its Drivers Aren't Core to Its Business, Won't Reclassify Them as Employees." *The Verge*. September 11. www.theverge.com/2019/9/11/20861362/uber-ab5-tony-west-drivers-core-ride-share-business-california.

Herrman, John. 2020. "All Your Favorite Brands, from BSTOEM to ZGGCD." *The New York Times*. February 11. www.nytimes.com/2020/02/11/style/amazon-trademark-copyright.html.

Hoberg, Gerard, and Gordon Phillips. 2016. "Text-Based Network Industries and Endogenous Product Differentiation." *Journal of Political Economy* 124(5):1423–65. doi: https://doi.org/10.1086/688176.

Hsieh, Chang-Tai, and Esteban Rossi-Hansberg. 2019. "The Industrial Revolution in Services." NBER Working Paper 25968.

Hubbard, Sally. 2020. *Monopolies Suck: 7 Ways Big Corporations Rule Your Life and How to Take Back Control.* New York: Simon & Schuster.

Jacobides, Michael G. 2005. "Industry Change through Vertical Disintegration: How and Why Markets Emerged in Mortgage Banking." *Academy of Management Journal* 48(3):465–98. doi: https://doi.org/10.5465/amj.2005.17407912.

Jensen, Michael C., and William H. Meckling. 1976. "Theory of the Firm: Managerial Behavior, Agency Costs and Ownership Structure." *Journal of Financial Economics* 3(4):305–60. doi: https://doi.org/10.1016/0304-405X(76)90026-X.

Kaiser Family Foundation. 2021. "2021 Employer Health Benefits Survey." November 10. www.kff.org/health-costs/report/2021-employer-health-benefits-survey/.

Kang, Cecilia. 2021. "Judge Throws out 2 Antitrust Cases against Facebook." *The New York Times.* June 28. www.nytimes.com/2021/06/28/technology/facebook-ftc-lawsuit.html.

Kaplow, Louis. 2013. "Market Definition: Impossible and Counterproductive." *Antitrust Law Journal* 79(1):361–79.

Kauffman Foundation. 2017. "2017 Startup Activity National Report Final." www.kauffman.org/wp-content/uploads/2019/09/2017_Kauffman_Index_Startup_Activity_National_Report_Final.pdf.

Kenney, Martin, and John Zysman. 2016. "The Rise of the Platform Economy." *Issues in Science and Technology* 32(3):61–69.

Khan, Lina. 2017. "Amazon's Antitrust Paradox." *Yale Law Journal* 126:710–805.

Khan, Lina, and Sandeep Vaheesan. 2017. "Market Power and Inequality: The Antitrust Counterrevolution and Its Discontents." *Harvard Law & Policy Review* 11:235–94.

Knoema. 2020. "Top Vehicle Manufacturers in the US Market, 1961–2016." May 21. https://knoema.com/infographics/floslle/top-vehicle-manufacturers-in-the-us-market-1961-2016.

Konczal, Mike. 2021. *Freedom from the Market: America's Fight to Liberate Itself from the Grip of the Invisible Hand.* New York: The New Press.

Kosciolek, Ashley. 2021. "Fact Check: Do Cruise Lines Pay US Taxes?" *Cruise Radio.Net.* July 13. https://cruiseradio.net/fact-check-do-cruise-lines-pay-us-taxes/.

Lamoreaux, Naomi R. 1985. *The Great Merger Movement in American Business, 1895–1904.* New York: Cambridge University Press.

Lamoreaux, Naomi R. 2019. "The Problem of Bigness: From Standard Oil to Google." *Journal of Economic Perspectives* 33(3):94–117. doi: https://doi.org/10.1257/jep.33.3.94.

Lewis, Paul. 2017. "'Our Minds Can Be Hijacked': The Tech Insiders Who Fear a Smartphone Dystopia." *The Guardian*. October 6. www.theguardian.com/technology/2017/oct/05/smartphone-addiction-silicon-valley-dystopia.

Lynn, Barry C. 2020. *Liberty from All Masters: The New American Autocracy vs. the Will of the People*. New York: St. Martin's Press.

Manjoo, Farhad. 2017. "The Hidden Player Spurring a Wave of Cheap Consumer Devices: Amazon." *The New York Times*. December 6. www.nytimes.com/2017/12/06/technology/cheap-consumer-devices-amazon.html.

Manne, Henry G. 1965. "Mergers and the Market for Corporate Control." *Journal of Political Economy* 73(2):110–20. doi: https://doi.org/10.1086/259000.

McGreal, Chris. 2019. "Capitalism Gone Wrong: How Big Pharma Created America's Opioid Carnage." *The Guardian*. July 24. www.theguardian.com/us-news/2019/jul/24/opioids-crisis-big-pharma-drugs-carnage.

McKinsey & Co. 2021. "McKinsey's Private Markets Annual Review." November 17. www.mckinsey.com/industries/private-equity-and-principal-investors/our-insights/mckinseys-private-markets-annual-review#.

Meagher, Michelle. 2020. *Competition Is Killing Us: How Big Business Is Harming Our Society and Planet – and What to Do about It*. London: Penguin Random House.

Montag, Ali. 2017. "The Instant Pot Is Selling like Crazy on Amazon – and Its PhD Inventor Says He's Read All 39,000 Reviews." *CNBC*. November 27. www.cnbc.com/2017/11/24/why-robert-wangs-instant-pot-is-a-bestseller-on-amazon.html.

Morozov, Evgeny. 2019. "Capitalism's New Clothes." *The Baffler*. February 4.

N, Arishekar. 2021. "Amazon Statistics (Seller, FBA, and Product) That'll Surprise You." *SellerApp*. November 22. www.sellerapp.com/blog/amazon-seller-statistics/.

Neate, Rupert. 2021. "Microsoft's Irish Subsidiary Posted £220bn Profit in Single Year." *The Guardian*. June 3. www.theguardian.com/world/2021/jun/03/microsoft-irish-subsidiary-paid-zero-corporate-tax-on-220bn-profit-last-year.

Neate, Rupert, and Dominic Rushe. 2021. "Google, Apple and Microsoft Report Record-Breaking Profits." *The Guardian*. July 27. www.theguardian.com/technology/2021/jul/27/google-apple-and-microsoft-to-report-record-breaking-profits.

Nelson, Eshe, and Jason Karaian. 2017. "Amazon Has Made Half the Profits of Macy's over the Past 20 Years." *Quartz*. July 28. https://qz.com/1040856/amazon-amzn-has-made-half-the-profits-of-macys-m-over-the-past-20-years/.

New York Times. 1972. "Papers Show I.T.T Urged U.S. to Help Oust Allende." *The New York Times*. July 3. www.nytimes.com/1972/07/03/archives/papers-show-itt-urged-us-to-help-oust-allende-suggestions-for.html.

Oremus, Will. 2021. "Lawmakers' Latest Idea to Fix Facebook: Regulate the Algorithm." *The Washington Post*. October 12. www.washingtonpost.com/technology/2021/10/12/congress-regulate-facebook-algorithm/.

Oreskes, Naomi, and Erik M. Conway. 2010. *Merchants of Doubt: How a Handful of Scientists Obscured the Truth on Issues from Tobacco Smoke to Global Warming*. New York: Bloomsbury Press.

Ovide, Shira. 2021. "The Limits of Facebook's 'Supreme Court'." *The New York Times*. May 5. www.nytimes.com/2021/05/05/technology/facebook-oversight-board-trump.html.

Paul, Sanjukta. 2020. "Antitrust as Allocator of Coordination Rights." *UCLA Law Review* 67(2):378. https://ssrn.com/abstract=3337861.

Paul, Sanjukta. 2021 "Recovering the Moral Economy Foundations of the Sherman Act." *Yale Law Journal* 131(1):175–255.

Plambeck, Erica L., and Lyn Denend. 2008. "The Greening of Wal-Mart." *Stanford Social Innovation Review* 6(2):52–59. https://ssir.org/articles/entry/the_greening_of_wal_mart.

Posner, Eric A., Glen Weyl, and Suresh Naidu. 2018. "Antitrust Remedies for Labor Market Power." *Harvard Law Review* 132:536–601.

Rahman, K. Sabeel. 2017. *Democracy against Domination*. New York: Oxford University Press.

Rekenthaler, John. 2019. "You're More Internationally Diversified Than You (Probably) Realize." *Morningstar, Inc*. February 22. www.morningstar.com/articles/914896/youre-more-internationally-diversified-than-you-probably-realize.

Richtel, Matt, and Andrew Jacobs. 2018. "American Adults Just Keep Getting Fatter." *The New York Times*. March 23. www.nytimes.com/2018/03/23/health/obesity-us-adults.html.

Robertson, Adi. 2020. "Trump Threatens That TikTok Will 'Close down' on September 15th Unless an American Company Buys It." *The Verge*. August 3. www.theverge.com/2020/8/3/21352878/trump-us-ban-tiktok-microsoft-acquisition-treasury-interview-deadline.

Romer, Paul. 2019. "A Tax That Could Fix Big Tech." *The New York Times*. May 6. www.nytimes.com/2019/05/06/opinion/tax-facebook-google.html.

Romer, Paul. 2021. "Why We Should Tax Digital Advertising." *Capitalisn't Podcast*, University of Chicago Booth School of Business. March 11. https:// review.chicagobooth.edu/economics/2021/article/capitalisn-t-why-we-should-tax-digital-advertising

Roose, Kevin. 2017. "Inside the Home of Instant Pot, the Kitchen Gadget That Spawned a Religion." *The New York Times*. December 17. www.nytimes .com/2017/12/17/business/instant-pot.html.

Rosenberg, Nathan, and Bryce Wilson Stucki. 2021. "Don't Trust the Antitrust Narrative on Farms." LPE Project. May 10. https://lpeproject.org/blog/dont-trust-the-antitrust-narrative-on-farms/.

Rossi-Hansberg, Esteban, Pierre-Daniel Sarte, and Nicholas Trachter. 2021. "Diverging Trends in National and Local Concentration." NBER Working Paper No. w25066. https://ssrn.com/abstract=3254041.

Roy, William G. 1999. *Socializing Capital: The Rise of the Large Industrial Corporation in America*. Princeton, NJ: Princeton University Press.

RSH Technologies. 2021. "What Is e-Residency: How to Start an EU Company Online." www.rsh.ee/what-is-e-residency-how-to-start-an-eu-company-online-in-estonia/.

Salam, Maya. 2017. "The Opioid Epidemic: A Crisis Years in the Making." *The New York Times*. October 27. www.nytimes.com/2017/10/26/us/opioid-crisis-public-health-emergency.html.

Sales, Nancy Jo. 2020. "How Juul Gets Kids Addicted to Vaping: It's Even Worse Than You Think." *The Guardian*. February 14. www.theguardian .com/commentisfree/2020/feb/14/juul-vape-smoking-e-cigarettes-health.

Schor, Juliet. 2020. *After the Gig: How the Sharing Economy Got Hijacked and How to Win It Back*. Oakland, CA: University of California Press.

Sedacca, Matthew, and David Yaffe-Bellany. 2019. "Cooking Eggs in the Morning and Shucking Oysters at Night, Thanks to an App." *The New York Times*. September 1. www.nytimes.com/2019/09/01/business/restaurant-jobs-apps.html.

Segal, David. 2021. "Has Online Retail's Biggest Bully Returned?" *The New York Times*. May 2. www.nytimes.com/2021/05/02/business/has-online-retails-biggest-bully-returned.html.

Shapiro, Carl. 2018. "Antitrust in a Time of Populism." *International Journal of Industrial Organization* 61:714–48. doi: https://doi.org/10.1016/j.ijindorg .2018.01.001.

Staffing Industry Analysts. 2021. "Uber to Close Its Uber Works Staffing Operations." www2.staffingindustry.com/Editorial/Daily-News/Uber-to-close-its-Uber-Works-staffing-operations-53856 (accessed November 27, 2021).

Statista. 2021. "Digital Cameras – United States." Statista Market Forecast. Accessed November 27, 2021. www.statista.com/outlook/cmo/consumer-electronics/tv-radio-multimedia/digital-cameras/united-states.

Steinbaum, Marshall. 2019. "Antitrust, the Gig Economy, and Labor Market Power." *Law and Contemporary Problems* 82(3):45–64.

Stigler Committee on Digital Platforms. 2019. "Stigler Committee on Digital Platforms: Final Report." www.chicagobooth.edu/-/media/research/stigler/pdfs/digital-platforms–committee-report–stigler-center.pdf.

Stoller, Matt. 2019. *Goliath: The 100-Year War between Monopoly Power and Democracy.* New York: Simon & Schuster.

Stoller, Matt, Sarah Miller, and Zephyr Teachout. 2020. "Addressing Facebook and Google's Harms through a Regulated Competition Approach." American Economic Liberties Project. www.economicliberties.us/wp-content/uploads/2020/04/Working-Paper-Series-on-Corporate-Power_2.pdf.

Subcommittee on Antitrust, Commercial and Administrative Law of the Committee on the Judiciary. 2020. "Investigation of Competition in Digital Markets: Majority Staff Report and Recommendations." https://judiciary.house.gov/uploadedfiles/competition_in_digital_markets.pdf?utm_campaign=4493-519.

Talbot, Peter. 2019. "Uber Launches an App to Connect Job Seekers with Gig Work." *National Public Radio.* October 3. www.npr.org/2019/10/03/766861700/uber-launches-an-app-to-connect-job-seekers-with-gig-work.

Teachout, Zephyr, and Lina Khan. 2014. "Market Structure and Political Law: A Taxonomy of Power." *Duke Journal of Constitutional Law & Public Policy* 9:37–74.

The White House. 2021. "Executive Order on Promoting Competition in the American Economy." Briefing. July 9. www.whitehouse.gov/briefing-room/presidential-actions/2021/07/09/executive-order-on-promoting-competition-in-the-american-economy/.

Thelen, Kathleen. 2018. "Regulating Uber: The Politics of the Platform Economy in Europe and the United States." *Perspectives on Politics* 16 (4):938–53. doi: https://doi.org/10.1017/S1537592718001081.

Thompson, Nicholas. 2018. "Inside the Two Years That Shook Facebook – and the World." *Wired.* February 12. www.wired.com/story/inside-facebook-mark-zuckerberg-2-years-of-hell/.

Urban Institute. 2021. Delaware. www.urban.org/policy-centers/cross-center-initiatives/state-and-local-finance-initiative/projects/state-fiscal-briefs/delaware.

US Census Bureau. 2017. "Startup Firms Created over 2 Million Jobs in 2015." October 8. www.census.gov/newsroom/press-releases/2017/business-dynamics.html.

Vatter, Ott. 2019. "Five Years of e-Residency: Past, Present and Future." *Medium*. December 16. https://medium.com/e-residency-blog/five-years-of-e-residency-past-present-and-future-3df1786aa5ca.

Wakabayashi, Daisuke. 2019. "Google's Shadow Work Force: Temps Who Outnumber Full-Time Employees." *The New York Times*. May 28. www.nytimes.com/2019/05/28/technology/google-temp-workers.html.

Weber, Klaus, Gerald F. Davis, and Michael Lounsbury. 2009. "Policy as Myth and Ceremony? The Global Spread of Stock Exchanges, 1980–2005." *Academy of Management Journal* 52(6):1319–47. doi: https://doi.org/10.5465/amj.2009.47085184.

Werden, Gregory J. 2014. "The Relevant Market: Possible and Productive." *Antitrust Law Journal Online*. www.americanbar.org/content/dam/aba/publishing/antitrust_law_journal/online-archive/werden-online-pdf.pdf.

Wheeler, Tom, Phil Verveer, and Gene Kimmelman. 2020. "New Digital Realities; New Oversight Solutions in the U.S.: The Case for a Digital Platform Agency and a New Approach to Regulatory Oversight." Shorenstein Center on Media, Politics and Public Policy, Harvard Kennedy School. August. https://shorensteincenter.org/wp-content/uploads/2020/08/New-Digital-Realities_August-2020.pdf.

White, Lawrence J. 2002. "Trends in Aggregate Concentration in the United States." *Journal of Economic Perspectives* 16(4):137–60.

White, Lawrence J., and Jasper Yang. 2020. "What Has Been Happening to Aggregate Concentration in the US Economy in the Twenty-First Century?" *Contemporary Economic Policy* 38(3):483–95. doi: https://doi.org/10.1111/coep.12460.

Wilmers, Nathan. 2018. "Wage Stagnation and Buyer Power: How Buyer–Supplier Relations Affect U.S. Workers' Wages, 1978 to 2014." *American Sociological Review* 83(2):213–42. doi: https://doi.org/10.1177/0003122418762441.

Wilson, Mark. 2020. "Car Design Is about to Change Forever. This Video Encapsulates How." *Fast Company*. October 11. www.fastcompany.com/90562654/car-design-is-about-to-change-forever-this-video-encapsulates-how.

Wolf, Martin. 2004. *Why Globalization Works*. New Haven, CT: Yale University Press.

Woo, Erin. 2021. "QR Codes Are Here to Stay. So Is the Tracking They Allow." *The New York Times*. July 26. www.nytimes.com/2021/07/26/technology/qr-codes-tracking.html.

Wu, Tim. 2018. *The Curse of Bigness: Antitrust in the New Gilded Age*. New York: Columbia Global Reports.

Zakrzewski, Cat. 2021. "Senators Aim to Block Tech Giants from Prioritizing Their Own Products over Rivals'." *The Washington Post*. October 14. www .washingtonpost.com/technology/2021/10/14/klobuchar-grassley-antitrust-bill/.

Zhang, Eva. 2021. "Startups Boom in the United States during Covid-19." Peterson Institute for International Economics. February 17. www.piie .com/blogs/realtime-economic-issues-watch/startups-boom-united-states-during-covid-19.

Zuboff, Shoshana. 2019. *The Age of Surveillance Capitalism: The Fight for a Human Future at the New Frontier of Power*. New York: PublicAffairs.

Cambridge Elements ⹁

Reinventing Capitalism

Arie Y. Lewin

Duke University, The Fuqua School of Business

Arie Y. Lewin is Professor Emeritus of Strategy and International Business at Duke University, Fuqua School of Business. He is an Elected Fellow of the Academy of International Business and a Recipient of the Academy of Management inaugural Joanne Martin Trailblazer Award. Previously, he was Editor-in-Chief of *Management and Organization Review* (2015–2021) and the *Journal of International Business Studies* (2000–2007), founding Editor-in-Chief of *Organization Science* (1989–2007), and Convener of Organization Science Winter Conference (1990–2012). His research centers on studies of organizations' adaptation as co-evolutionary systems, the emergence of new organizational forms, and adaptive capabilities of innovating and imitating organizations. His current research focuses on de-globalization and decoupling, the Fourth Industrial Revolution, and the renewal of capitalism.

Till Talaulicar

University of Erfurt, Germany

Till Talaulicar holds the Chair of Organization and Management at the University of Erfurt where he is also the Dean of the Faculty of Economics, Law and Social Sciences. His main research expertise is in the areas of corporate governance and the responsibilities of the corporate sector in modern societies. Professor Talaulicar is Editor-in-Chief of *Corporate Governance: An International Review*, Senior Editor of *Management and Organization Review* and serves on the Editorial Board of *Organization Science*. Moreover, he has been Founding Member and Chairperson of the Board of the International Corporate Governance Society (2014–2020).

Editorial Advisory Board

Tsuyoshi Numagami, *Hitotsubashi University, Japan*
Margit Osterloh, *University of Basel, Switzerland*
Andreas Georg Scherer, *University of Zurich, Switzerland*
Blair Sheppard, *PwC, USA*
Jeffrey Sonnenfeld, *Yale University, USA*
John Sutton, *LSE, UK*
David Teece, *UC Berkeley, USA*
Anne S. Tsui, *University of Notre Dame, USA*
Alain Verbeke, *University of Calgary, Canada*
Henk Volberda, *University of Amsterdam, The Netherlands*
Mira Wilkins, *Florida International University, USA*
Sarah Williamson, *FCLTGlobal, USA*
Arjen van Witteloostuijn, *VU Amsterdam, The Netherlands*
George Yip, *Imperial College London, UK*

About the Series

This series seeks to feature explorations about the crisis of legitimacy facing capitalism today, including the increasing income and wealth gap, the decline of the middle class, threats to employment due to globalization and digitalization, undermined trust in institutions, discrimination against minorities, global poverty and pollution. Being grounded in a business and management perspective, the series incorporates contributions from multiple disciplines on the causes of the current crisis and potential solutions to renew capitalism.

Panmure House is the final and only remaining home of Adam Smith, Scottish philosopher and 'Father of modern economics.' Smith occupied the House between 1778 and 1790, during which time he completed the final editions of his master works: *The Theory of Moral Sentiments* and *The Wealth of Nations*. Other great luminaries and thinkers of the Scottish Enlightenment visited Smith regularly at the House across this period. Their mission is to provide a world-class 21st-century centre for social and economic debate and research, convening in the name of Adam Smith to effect positive change and forge global, future-focussed networks.

ADAM SMITH
PANMURE
HOUSE

Cambridge Elements $\equiv$

Reinventing Capitalism

Printed in the United States
by Baker & Taylor Publisher Services